Keepers of the Light
A History of the St. Marks Lighthouse and the Gresham Family

by
Myrna Roberts Kanekkeberg

Typeface: Times New Roman

Printing and binding by Durraprint

Library of Congress Control Number: 2010942043

ISBN 10: 1-889574-40-6
ISBN 13: 978-1-889574-40-0

Sentry Press
424 East Call Street
Tallahassee, Florida 32301
(850) 224-7423

TABLE OF CONTENTS

<u>DEDICATION</u>

This book is dedicated to my mother, Vera Gresham Roberts, for her unique ability to shine a light on the everyday experience and make it come to life. It is with gratitude that she is able to share this with those of us who long for a simpler and more romantic time.

PREFACE

This book is the story of the St. Marks Lighthouse, Florida's second oldest. It has been in operation since 1829-1830 and is one of the most beautiful in the United States. In 1837 a new light was constructed and a third one farther inland the same year. It stands today as an outpost on the Gulf of Mexico and is located in North Florida's Wakulla County on sugar white sand spits, surrounded on the north by marshy ponds. On the south side is the Gulf of Mexico and the mouth of the St. Marks River, whose entry and exit was ovresoon by the light and its custodians for many years. It is a natural and semi-wild setting of animal, bird, and marine life varying from sea turtles to rattlesnakes and of bird life from soaring ospreys, eagles, egrets, great blue herons, ducks, owls, red-winged blackbirds, and all sorts of smaller song birds.

This history centers mainly around the human story of one family, the Greshams, whose various members go back in time for fifty-seven years. The readers of this book will find themselves reminded of Johann Rudolph Wyss's earlier nineteenth century adventure novel, *Swiss Family Robinson*, about a shipwrecked family on a desert island. Although one story is fiction and this one is true, both evoke an overwhelming sense of nature's beauty, force, and ever-changing whims and wonders.

This book also documents the history of the area dating back to the Spanish settlements in St. Marks and includes the other early lighthouse keepres and their families from the light's first operations in the 1820's until World War II when the United States Coast Guard assumed military command.

The work also makes a major historical contribution by documenting the lives and livelihoods of many pioneers in Wakulla, Leon, and surrounding areas. It documents the many visitors and friends of the Greshams--their parties, picnics, and gathings of many kinds are countless.

Keepers of the Light is the carefully documented work of a brother-sister team: Myrna Roberts Kanekkeberg and John Y. Roberts. They began as a writing team; however, they later decided that

Myrna should do most of the writing, while John, who lives in Tallahassee, was better able to do the research needed. Their residences were also a factor, since Myrna lives in Washington State--quite a distance from John. John is with the Federal Bureau of Investigation and was able to access the National Archives in Washington, D.C. on one of his many trips there. In this way he provided valuable information from the logbooks, but was also able to obtain information from the Florida Archives in Tallahassee.

Both writers are deeply knowledgeable of the North Florida region. John is a graduate of Florida State University, while Myrna's education was business oriented. They have dedicated themselves to years of work in producing this history. The result is a highly readable, accurate, documented, informative, and fascinating history of the St. Marks Lighthouse, the people who lived there, and the surrounding region.

The thousands who have visited the lighthouse and the surrounding St. Marks Wildlife Refuge, established by the US government in 1932 with Paul Kaeger as Manager, have been impressed by the surrounding wilderness terrain, twenty miles south of Tallahassee, and easily reached by paved highway. It was not always so easily accessible. Securing supplies and other necessaries had to be done by means of a launch to the nearby and ancient mainland village of St. Marks. A highway to the light was not constructed until 1931. It was built by one of President Roosevelt's New Deal agencies, the Works Progress Administration (WPA). There was no electricity until 1939, although radio was available from about 1920.

The history recounts life it as was lived in this primitive and isolated, but beautiful North Florida region. The people lived in the crowded conditions of the tower home and maintained its efficiency and records and themselves. They experienced the rigors, tribulations, and pleasures of territorial and antebellum Florida, survived the strains of the Civil War, and the slow recovery from the war and economic bad times that the state experienced in the last half of the nineteenth century. Then came the twentieth century and World War I followed by a decade of prosperity that collapsed into the Great Depression of the thirties. It was followed by World War II when the people of the Gulf coast experienced the apprehensions and uncertainties to the dangers of Nazi submarines.

In the aftermath of postwar prosperity, Florida increased in population, accompanied by the growth of cities, industry, and tourism, along with continued growth of agriculture, cattle, and timber. Fishing, both commercial and recreational, remained important. Coastal Florida's position as a vacation destination for tourists became international, and Florida shifted its status from an agrarian dominated economy to an urban controlled one.

Through it all, the St. Marks lighthouse carved its way through time, changing with the seasons, sometimes calmly, sometimes with the ferocity of summer hurricanes when winds and waves spent their fury destroying keeperss' carefully tended gardens and fruit trees; drowning their pets, fowl, and domestic animals. The light's custodians often took refuge in the tower. After the storm passed, and once the clouds cleared and life was calm again, there remained the knowledge and awe of nature's power.

There was work to be done and the keeper's responsibilities to be carried out. The families turned their confined quarters into wonders of space management and productive activities. In the early days there was a time when all of the Young and Lela Gresham's eight children were at home with only four rooms and a two-seat outhouse. Chores had to be done. Food was both store-purchased and home-grown, and it was abundant--supplemented by wildlife and domestic animals. There were vegetables, fruits, and berries in ample supply. Oaks, magnolias, and other trees dotted the grounds.

There was an ever-growing increase in visitors to the lighthouse, and constant repairs and repainting projects. There were also problems of building a seawall and coping with beach erosion. Traffic on the river, both recreational and commercial, was constant. It included fishermen and spongers.

There were wrecks and rescues, an occasional drowning, and sightseers and campers, young and old of all sexes and ages. With the building of the road meant more visitors, some as unusual as a group of Eskimos who came in 1931 with their winter clothing and dogs, only to move mysteriously on without a trace.

The skies were full of wonders. The Greshams were excited to see the dirigible *Shennandoah* fly silently over in September 1915 and saddened by its wreckage and loss of life later that same month in Pennsylvania. From Tallahassee, Ivan Munroe, local pioneer airman, was always a welcome sight when he landed his biplane *Ol' Hon* on the beach.

John Young Gresham retired in 1949. The lighthouse remained under the control of the United States Coast Gaurd, rotating keepers every two years. Their son, Alton, was in the Coast Guard at the time and took over as the first Officer in Charge from 1949 to 1951. The term "keeper" was no longer used as Coast Guardsmen took turns caring for the logging and was replaced by "Officer in Charge."

The lighthouse ceased being manned sometime in 1960 and has been on automatic ever since. In recent years, the Coast Guard Auxiliary used the house to operate radio equipment, but they have since departed.

William Warren Rogers
Professor Emeritus of History, Florida State University
and Director, Sentry Press, Inc.

ACKNOWLEDGEMENTS

This book would not have been possible without the many contributions of others. Most of my endeavors involved organizing material already on hand. This was no small task, as there was so much to choose from, but my creative efforts were minimal.

I would first like to acknowledge Dr. William Rogers, Director of the Sentry Press, not only for his faith in my abilities, but because I recognized in him a kindred soul whose interest in this rich historical area was evident from the beginning. Dr. Rogers is a Professor Emeritis of Florida State University in Tallahassee, Florida, and is the author of many historical books.

I would also like to acknowledge Karen Towson who worked with me in editing this book. She certainly qualifies as "one of Dr. Rogers' "geniuses", as he calls his staff. Karen has been a big help in guiding me through the publication process.

My brother, John Roberts, had originally planned to co-write this book, but since I'm in the Northwest and he's on the opposite side of the country in Tallahassee, he decided it would be easier for me to author the book. However, I must give him credit for all his efforts towards its successful publication. His contributions include the Introduction and an article entitled "The Magnolia Tree". He researched the logbooks at the National Archives while on assignment in Washington, DC for the FBI. He also researched the Florida Archives in Tallahassee, giving me a wealth of information. Because of his efforts, I was able to include some of the more interesting log entries that give authenticity to life at the lighthouse. Beyond all of these contributions, he has been very helpful in maintaining the connection I need with Professor Rogers.

John is a true historian and is active with the Wakulla County Historical Society. Through his contributions to that organization he has established an anticipation for the publication of this book. This is probably his greatest attribute–a genuine love of the Wakulla-Leon County area and its people.

I would also like to thank Aunt Edna (Edna Gresham Lambert) for her memories of life at the lighthouse. She was most helpful in describing the daily life of the four younger girls.

Aunt Dorothy, (Dorothy Gresham Prater) was very helpful in identifying some of the pictures from Mother's old photo album. She not only remembered who some of the people were, but had some interesting comments about them, as well.

Mother was my greatest contributor. This amuses me, since long before she passed away I had asked her to help in writing a book on the lighthouse. She declined. Nevertheless, she had told me many stories about her life there and had written down many accounts of her experiences, which I have included in this book. So, in a way, Mother helped me write this book after all!

I must give credit to my husband, George Kanekkeberg, as my technical advisor. Since I am computer illiterate, and he is an electronic whiz, there were many trips to the garage or the yard or where he was in his comfy chair watching television with questions about why the computer was doing this or that. He was also very helpful in setting up programs to make my job easier. I also want to thank him for the chaos he had to share in our work room. I'm very grateful for his (sometimes) great patience!

Finally, I want to extend a special "thank you" to the artist who provided the beautiful cover picture, Russell Grace, of Russell Grace Images, Tallahassee, Florida.

INTRODUCTION
By John Roberts

For as long as I can remember, I have had a fascination wtih history. My reading habits were centered on that subject from my elementary school days at the University School (Florida High School) in Tallahassee. The library there contained a series of biographies on famous Americans such as our founding fathers, past presidents, etc. I read them all as well as a series of fiction books authored by Joseph Altsheler pertaining to the opening of the frontier in the early American midwest.

After becoming aware that my forbears, particularly my father's paternal and maternal grandfathers had fought in regiments from Mississippi during the war between the states, throughout the rest of my life, to the present time, my focus has been on that period of our history.

As I matured, I also became very much interested in the history of the St. Marks Lighthouse in Florida, where our family had been lighthouse keepers for a combined period of 57 years. Those keepers were Charles Oliver Fine, great grandfather, following his death at the lighthouse, his wife, our great grandmother, Sarah Jane Fine, their son-in-law, our grandfather, John Young Gresham, and his son, our uncle, Alton T. Gresham.

My sister, Myrna Roberts Kanekkeberg, shared my love for, and interest in, our old family home, the St. Marks Lighthouse. Although I had many memories of life at the lighthouse, Myrna had retained more as she is four years older than I, and I was relatively young when our family ceased keeping the lighthouse.

After graduating from the Florida State Univeristy with a degree in Criminology, and entering upon a career as a Special Agent with the Naval Investigative Service (NCIS) and becoming a professional member of the law enforcement/intelligence community, my work ethic became one of gathering factual information. Assumptions and even opinions simply did not count as our final product had to withstand the scrutiny of the courts.

I began to learn that our history too often had no such requirement. It is so sad for such an important discipline that some who profess to be "experts" in historical matters are nothing of the sort. My purpose is not to ridicule so many who are honest, professional historians who work so very hard at research so as to provide accurate accounts of our history. What I'm trying to convey here has been immortalized in the words of Virginian Thomas Jefferson and used as the motto of the Wakulla County (Fl) Historical Society of which I am a proud member, "A Morsel of Genuine History is a Thing So Rare as to be Always Valuable".

I found especially and personally troubling the obvious errors in information regarding the history of the St. Marks Lighthouse. Dates of service of the various keepers were inaccurate, as well as other aspects, such as incorrect identification of photographs displayed of former residents, including my mother. Most shocking, was when during a tour of the lighthouse, the guide announced that my great grandfather, Charles Fine, had been killed and devoured by an alligator. I do not fault the guide in this case, since he had "documentary evidence" in the form of a pamphlet issued by the Florida Lighthouse Association. The pamphlet went on to report Mr. Fine is the only lighthouse keeper to have met his demise in that manner in U.S. history. I discreetly informed the guide of his error and soon thereafter also informed the Florida Lighthouse Association, and I believe they corrected the pamphlet. The fact is that Charles Fine died at the lighthouse of natural causes and this day rests peacefully in a cemetery at Wakulla Station, Florida.

To conclude, when I informed my sister, Myrna, she too was very upset, and we embarked upon the writing of this book. In that regard, I did some research at the National Archives in Washington, DC as well as the State Archives of Florida in Tallahassee. We first tried to share in the writing of our book, but found this to be awkward in that we live in exact opposite sections of the country—she in the northwest and me in the southeast. So my dear sister Myrna accepted the chore of compiling so much varied information into what we hope is an interesting, informative book concerning keepers of the light.

It is out hope and prayer that as to the extent possible, we have been true to the works of Thomas Jefferson, and if errors in history are noted, to encourage another to continue the task of researching and reporting the factual history of the place we love so much, the St. Marks Lighthouse.

PROLOGUE

Imagine every time you went to see your grandparents it was to a lighthouse overlooking the Gulf of Mexico, a paradise of birds, trees and alligators. It was a magical place with the smell of salt marsh and sudden squalls that blew in off the Gulf. The lights out on the water at night, along with the rhythmic flash from the tower and little bright eyes at the kitchen door—raccoons who loved Granddaddy's fig trees—were just a few examples of its mysterious charm. The memory of it compels us, my brother and I, to share with you this beautiful place.

A lighthouse is more than a home. Much like the castles of antiquity, these structures have had a far greater purpose which make them unique. As castles were intended primarily for defense, so the lighthouse has been dedicated to men of the sea and to their safety. And though castles are now simply beautiful monuments to the past, the lighthouse still shines its light across the waters each night. It is true, sadly, that it is now no more than a beacon. But there was a time in our living memory when it was a way of life.

Visible for 15 miles across the Gulf of Mexico, the lighthouse is located at the mouth of the St. Marks River. It has been in operation since 1829 and is the second oldest lighthouse in Florida, located in an area rich with history. As a boy, John, working as a helper on the *Jenny Lee*, remembers seeing that pretty tower as he returned from a hard day's work out on the fishing grounds. The sight of that tower taking shape over the homeward bound bow of the boat signaled the long day was almost over, and on those occasions when the sea was fierce and dangerous, it was an even more welcome sight.

The St. Marks lighthouse is situated in Wakulla County in the heart of the St. Marks Wildlife Refuge. It is approximately 20 miles south of the capital city, Tallahassee. To go there, take Highway 363 out of Tallahassee. As you head south, turn left (or east) onto U.S. 98 until you pass the town of New Port where you will cross the St. Marks River. Just beyond you will take the lighthouse road to the right. A few miles down the road you will enter the St. Marks

Wildlife Refuge. At this point a nominal fee is required for entry. Be sure to stop and browse through the small gift shop and see the instructional displays and pamphlets. Don't forget to pick up information on the many trails located along the remaining winding road. Take your time, for part of the pleasure is the trip, itself. Watch for the many exotic birds—egrets and cormorants; also eagles and ospreys and their nests which are visible in the tops of many of the tall cypress trees you will see along the way. Keep an eye out, also, for the lazy alligator sunning himself on the banks of the ditches near the ponds. Or you may catch a glimpse of a pair of eyes just over the water as he silently searches for unsuspecting prey. There is the occasional deer, and the black panther of Florida, though rarely seen, is also a native to the area. Small animals include the raccoon and opossum, as well as the many shore birds and seagulls. There are reptiles, besides the alligator, but they are seldom seen, and most of these are harmless.

Besides the animals and birds of the area, you will notice the varied trees—cypress, pine, magnolia and, of course, our state tree, the sable palm. As you continue the winding road, you will notice trails for hiking and lookout platforms along the way. Finally, you will come to a cross road. To the left was once the headquarters and home of the refuge manager. It was located on the mounds, which were once Indian burial grounds. Straight ahead is Mounds Pond where there are picnic tables, a fire tower, as well as another trail and scenic lookout platform. As you turn to the right, the trees fall away, the marshland blends with the silvery water and sky beyond, and there at the end of the road is the lighthouse.

The St. Marks Lighthouse.

The St. Marks Lighthouse, rear view.

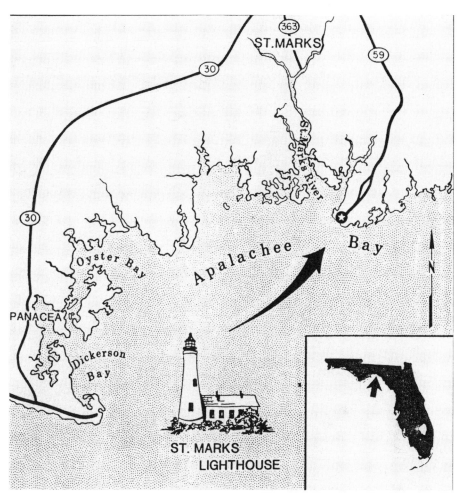

Map of Apalachee Bay.

Chapter 1
<u>EARLY HISTORY</u>

So why was there a need for a lighthouse in this particular place? Had you continued on south from Tallahassee by way of Route 363, you would have come to the small village of St. Marks. The road ends at the St. Marks River. Just to the west, about a mile, is the "Old Fort", or The Fort San Marcos de Apalache, located at the confluence of the St. Marks and Wakulla Rivers. This provided a natural promontory facing the Gulf beyond.

View of confluence of St. Marks and Wakulla rivers looking towards Gulf from Fort San Marcos de Apalache.

Florida has many underground rivers, and at the headwaters of the Wakulla River is Wakulla Springs, one of the largest springs in the world. The St. Marks River begins its journey in the north at Natural Bridge. Beyond the Fort towards the Gulf, the merging rivers become one—The St. Marks River.

It was at the fort that an early settlement was established by the Spanish. The founding date of the settlement probably occurred on the feast day of San Marcos, as that name was applied to both the town and the river—later Anglicized. The fort was crucial for protecting the power of, first Spain, England, the United States and, finally, the Confederacy. The fort was necessary, especially during the Spanish reign, to protect the string of Spanish missions which stretched from St. Augustine over towards Pensacola. Before they built the lighthouse, legend has it that the Spaniards would hang big streamers or banners in the trees near where the lighthouse is now so that their ships could easily locate the mouth of the St. Marks River.

In 1828, William P. Duval, who succeeded Andrew Jackson as governor of the Florida Territory, encouraged Joseph M. White, a territorial delegate to congress, to petition for the construction of a lighthouse at St. Marks. White contacted the chair of the Senate Committee on Commerce with the plea, and on May 23, 1828, an act appropriating $6,000 for the construction of the St. Marks Lighthouse was passed.

The contract for the lighthouse was awarded to Winslow Lewis, and under his direction, Benjamin Beal and Jairus Thayer constructed a tower at a cost of $11,765. However, the collector of customs for St. Marks refused to accept the lighthouse, as it was built with hollow walls, a practice that was not yet widely accepted. Calvin Knowlton, Lewis' partner, supervised the construction of a solid replacement tower, which was accepted in January of 1830.

In 1837, the Tallahassee-St. Marks Railroad, one of Florida's oldest, was completed. The 20-mile line was conceived and financed by plantation owners to aid in transporting their cotton crops to the port of St. Marks. There were several large storage areas along the railroad in St. Marks in those days where cotton and other items were stored awaiting shipment to western destinations along the Gulf. (Cipra and McCarthy)

By 1843, the railroad had been extended across the river a short distance east of the fort. The reason for this was that the St. Marks port was busy and narrow, so that it was decided that the little outpost community of Port Leon, settled around 1838, would better serve as a distribution center. It was also conceived to be profitable from leases and the sale of lots in the new development.

In less than five years Port Leon had reached the small town class in resident population. The business interests were largely maritime. Dockage and warehouses were built, as well as homes, general stores and two taverns. There was even a small weekly paper. The buildings were of frame construction and the highest elevation in town was only a few feet.

On September 13, 1843, the wind commenced blowing from the southeast bringing up a high tide. Late in the afternoon the wind lulled and the tide fell. By about 11:00 p.m., the wind again strengthened and by midnight the gale had increased alarmingly approaching hurricane force. As the wind increased, it drove a tidal wave ashore to a depth of seven to ten feet. The wind continued unabated until 2:00 a.m. on the morning of the 14th, when the wind suddenly abated as the eye of the hurricane passed over. Then, in a few minutes, the winds began blowing from the southwest with renewed violence.

Every dwelling house and store that was not demolished was left in a shattered and filthy condition. Miraculously, there was only one death in Port Leon, a young black boy who drowned.

The citizens of Port Leon decided to abandon the area and move to another location. They chose what is now New Port located about four miles upriver above St. Marks. (Davis, Vol. 24)

The hurricane took down the bridge that crossed the river at St. Marks and inflicted substantial damage to that town, also.

By 1842, erosion was threatening the lighthouse, and a new lighthouse was erected farther inland. The third St. Marks lighthouse, which still stands today resting on a base of limestone rocks taken from Fort San Marcos de Apalache, was originally 65 feet tall. The walls are four feet thick at the bottom and taper to a thickness of 18 inches at the top. The sturdy construction probably saved the lives of the Mungerfords, the keeper and his family at the time of the 1843 hurricane. (Cipra and McCarthy)

Tallahassee *Star of Florida,* March 31, 1842
"Notice to Mariners, Collector's Office
…St. Marks Lighthouse pulled down to make room for a new one, now in progress, and the contract to be completed by first day of June next. W.B. Ware, superintendent of St. Marks lighthouse."

Chapter 2
EARLY LIGHTHOUSE KEEPERS/
THE CIVIL WAR

Some of the following tenure dates of the keepers vary slightly with other less reliable sources of information. We will only be concerned with those dates recorded in the national archives.

The first lighthouse keeper was Samuel Crosby (1830-1839).

Under the 1832 Treaty of Payne's Landing, Florida's Seminole Indians were to relocate west of the Mississippi River by 1835. However, when 1835 arrived, the Indians refused to leave, and the Second Seminole Indian War, which would last for seven years, erupted. During the first two years of the war, the lighthouses at Mosquito Inlet and Cape Florida were attacked. Fearing for the safety of his family, Keeper Crosby requested that a detachment of soldiers be stationed near the St. Marks Lighthouse. His request was denied. Crosby then asked for an escape boat that he could use in case of an attack, but again his petition was not granted. Fortunately, no attack was made on the St. Marks lighthouse during Crosby's tenure. (Cipra and McCarthy)

(NOTE): John, in his research in the Florida Archives in Tallahassee, discovered some interesting articles regarding the early days at the lighthouse, included here.

The Magnolia Advisor, March 13, 1830
"We take pleasure in announcing to the Masters of vessels and others interested the lighthouse at the mouth of the harbour is completed and in operation. The difficulties and delays so long complained of in finding the entrance to the harbour are entirely obviated. It forms a conspicuous beacon by day and the light is represented to be excellent."

Tallahassee *Floridian and Journal*, August 31, 1830
"St. Marks Lighthouse—The lighthouse is becoming a

place of considerable resort to those in pursuit of health or amusement. Fishing, fowling, the sea-bath and breezes are no small attractions these dull piping times."

Tallahassee *Floridian*, December 27, 1831
Custom House Magnolia
"December 26, 1831 Sealed proposals will be received until the 1st day of February next, for white washing the tower of the St. Marks Lighthouse—for placing two spar buoys in the harbor—Jessie H. Willis, Collector"

Benjamin Metcalf (1839-1841), maintained the light following Crosby.

Captain J.P. Hungerford (1841-1844), whose family survived the terrible hurricane of 1843, followed Metcalf.

Captain Hungerford and his family survived the storm surge of the hurricane of 1843 by climbing up the tower to the landing just below the housing. Fifteen others in the dwelling drowned.

Port Leon *Gazette*, September 15, 1843
"…but our losses (Port Leon and St. Marks) are nothing compared with those at the Lighthouse. Every building but the lighthouse is gone, and dreadful to relate, fourteen lives were lost. Some of them were our most valued citizens. We cannot attempt to estimate the loss of each individual at this time but shall reserve it until our feelings will better enable us to investigate it. Below we give a list of drowned, as far as heard from…at the Lighthouse: Capt. M.C. Robertson, his wife and three children and a child of Dr. Tradewell's; Mr. J. Wood, a portrait painter from Tallahassee; a child of R.V. Buffin's and five Negroes. Those saved at the Lighthouse: Capt. Hungerford, his wife and two children, Dr. Tradewell's youngest child; Messrs. Oglesbee, Blethen, and Kennedy, pilots and five Negroes." (*Magnolia Monthly*, II, No. 5)

Needham Dudley (1844-1850) was the Keeper when Florida became a state in 1845, followed by his wife, Mrs. Ann Dudley (1850-1854) upon his death.

Ann Dudley was the first of two women keepers in St. Marks, the second being our great grandmother, Sarah Fine.

"[Lighthouse keepers] were permitted to pursue other jobs, such as fishing or piloting ships into harbors or farming. Members of their families, including wives and daughters, learned to keep the lights burning when their men were away. When a male keeper fell ill or died, many of these women simply took over their husband's or father's duties, often receiving official appointments because there was no pension system to care for them." (Clifford and Clifford 2)

During Mrs. Dudley's tenure three large hurricanes hit the lighthouse in the 1850s. One destroyed the 160 foot long sea wall, six feet thick and ten feet high that had been built in 1844. In the 1851 storm, Ann Dudley lost almost all her worldly possessions totaling around $1,100. Her petition to Congress for compensation went unheeded. (Cipra and McCarthy)

Tallahassee *Florida Sentinel*, October 12, 1852
"Destructive Storm—St. Marks and Newport
The lighthouse is badly damaged, though not destroyed. The breakwater is in good part gone. The iron door is carried away, and the building strained, contents gone, will need immediate attention. The keeper's house is nearly all destroyed, and all her furniture, clothing, bedding, provisions, etc., lost"

The house was eventually replaced in 1854, along with a new seawall. (Cipra and McCarthy)

David Kennedy, (1855-1880), was the keeper during the Civil War.

There is a small chip on the lens, and great grandfather Fine, who was keeper less than 30 years after the Civil War, said that the keeper of the light, apparently, Kennedy, observed preparations being made by sailors from the Yankee blockading fleet to come ashore at the lighthouse. He then removed the very valuable lens from the tower and hid with it in the marsh grass out on the sand flats near the lighthouse. Those lens were heavy, and while he and a Confederate soldier were carrying them down the winding stairs, they dropped the lens, thereby chipping it. This is only hearsay and could be untrue. However, it has been widely reported over the years.

On June 15, 1862, the *USS Tahoma*…and *USS Somerset*… crossed the bar of the St. Marks River and shelled the confederate fort near the lighthouse for 40 minutes. The artillery company stationed there withdrew, and sailors landed and destroyed the battery and burned the buildings used as barracks. (*Civil War Naval Chronology* 69, 167)

(NOTE:) The battery mentioned above is Fort Williams, believed to be located at what was later called "Countryman's Hill".

By 1844, Pensacola to the west and St. Marks to the east were shipping rivals. In February and March, 1865, the blockading force was increased off Apalachicola, and most of these units were sent to St. Marks with the intent to take Natural Bridge. The plan was to move by land and water against St. Marks from the lighthouse on Apalachee Bay. In a combined effort, ships would ascend the St. Marks River while soldiers would proceed overland to New Port, seize the bridge, and take St. Marks from the rear. They would then cut the railroad to Tallahassee. Although the plan was sound, it failed because the ships were unable to reach

Civil War monument located at Natural Bridge in Woodville, Leon County, Florida.

their destination upriver. Thus, the troops on foot were forced into battle north of New Port at Natural Bridge where they were defeated. (Rogers 10 and 85)

During the Civil War, widows were absorbed into households, sometimes as paid servants. One such lady, Georgianna Barbara Lane McSwain, was taken in by Dr. Charles A. Hentz of Quincy, paying her a monthly wage to assist with housekeeping chores. He described her as "a fat, dumpy, good-natured widow" who helped his wife and daughters and later married the lighthouse keeper at St. Marks. Unfortunately, the keeper was not identified.

On rare occasions, women emerged as victors, manipulating convention and winning small triumphs.

"On July 5, 1861, Lt. J.H. Strong of the *USS Mohawk*, took his first prize, the sloop *George B. Sloat*, which tried to run the blockade at the mouth of the St. Marks River. It was customary to seize the flag of the apprehended ship, but 'the lady...of Adjutant General Holland of Florida' was on board with her three children and two slaves. She quickly 'claimed the flag to be her personal property and secured it to her person.' Strong faced a dilemma; taking the flag would entail undressing the lady. Later Mrs. Holland agreed that Strong behaved as a gentleman, taking her family on his gunboat before he scuttled the *Sloat*. She was delivered under a flag of truce to Fort Williams. She eventually returned to Tallahassee, and the next morning, the Fourth Florida Regiment drew up in line in front of the hotel and presented arms; they had no flag, so Mrs. Holland gave them the one she had worn." (Revels 71, 127)

There is an historical marker, one of many erected in Wakulla County by The History Committee, St. Marks Waterfront Florida Partnership, describing the Steamship *Spray* which played a significant role during the Civil War. This particular marker, funded by Shields Marina in St Marks, gives a brief history of the *Spray*, and is located across the road from the St. Marks Baptist Church.

STEAMSHIP *SPRAY*
1850-1872

"The steamship *Spray*, a wood-burning, 118 ton side-wheel steamer was owned primarily by Daniel Ladd, the richest merchant on the St. Marks River. The ship transported goods and passengers between St. Marks and oceangoing vessels as well as playing a significant role during the Civil War. The *Spray* traveled to Cedar Key, up the Suwannee River, to Columbus, Georgia and as far west as New Orleans.

"The steamship *Spray* was an important vessel along the St. Marks River for many years. When Daniel Ladd purchased a two-thirds share of the ship in 1850, it was to be used as both a towboat and to transport people and goods from St. Marks to vessels anchored in deep water near the mouth of the river in an area called Spanish Hole. The *Spray*, with 70 horsepower, a walking beam, a white smokestack and a single mast, averaged 12 knots an hour on the open sea. It could go downriver from Ladd's home in Newport to St. Marks in time to meet the train from Tallahassee, take passengers, mail and cargo out to ships anchored at Spanish Hole and bring other passengers, mail and freight back to meet the return train to Tallahassee before proceeding back to Newport—all in a single day.

"By April 1864, the steamship *Spray* was commandeered by the confederate Navy, commanded by H.H. Lewis, and had two guns. It guarded the mouth of the river, was chased and received a few hits, but survived. Ladd owned the iron works in Newport that repaired steam boilers for ships as well as sawmill engines. This was a confederate advantage during the Civil War because confederate ships could run the blockade while Yankee ships headed to Hilton Head or New York City for repairs. When the Yankees attempted to take the capital of Florida, the cannons at the fort and the *Spray* were guarding the river. The federal troops were forced to march up the east side of the river to Natural Bridge where confederate troops forced a retreat. Tallahassee was never controlled by federal troops until the city was surrendered at the end of the war. Although the *Spray* was captured and taken to the Union port of Key West, she was returned to Ladd after the war. Ladd again transported goods and passengers along the St. Marks River until his death in 1872 and soon after, the *Spray* sank from neglect."

(NOTE:) Mr. Ladd was a prominent citizen originally of Port Leon until the hurricane of 1843, and later of New Port. He was instrumental in establishing New Port as one of the largest and most commercially successful Florida towns at that time. See Jerrell A. Shofner's book, *Daniel Ladd, Merchant Prince of Frontier Florida* (Gainesville, FL, 1978).

After the war the tower and keeper's house were repaired, and received a new fourth-order Fresnel lens, which was lit by Keeper David Kennedy on January 7, 1867. In 1883, the tower was extended an additional ten feet, raising its focal plane to 80 feet.

In 1873 yet another hurricane forced the family into the tower where they survived the night. Later repairs were undertaken to the house and tower. (Cipra and McCarthy)

(NOTE): According to my brother, John, lighthouse logs were mandated by the United States Lighthouse Service (USLHS) beginning around 1870. Some of the more interesting of these entries will be interspersed throughout the text to give credence to the lighthouse keepers' daily life. Grammatical errors are left intact just as the keepers wrote them.

April 22, 1872, David M. Kennedy, Keeper "…hail storm, thunder lightning and rain. Hail stones large as ounce balls, fresh breeze from SE to NW, all ronde [sic] the cumpis.[sic]"

February 2, 1880, Kennedy, Keeper "...a wild duck broke through one of the storm paines [sic] 12 o'clock at night had to prop it with a plank."

June 2, 1880, Kennedy, Keeper "...Light tender *Arbutus* came in to make repairs to dwelling and began putting up new chimney on kitchen which was destroyed by the recent tornado, also began putting on new shutters on the tower..."

June 18, 1880, Kennedy, Keeper "...Captain Bryson anchored in Spanish Hole with his crew and white washed the tower and dwelling inside and out and repaired the weather gutters and the pump. Made a very nise [sic] job of hit [sic].

There were many entries in Kennedy's log book regarding problems with oil leaks in the lamp and resulting in a dim light or the light would go out. Some nights he reported sitting up in the tower most of the night, watching the lamp so that it wouldn't go out. After a considerable amount of time, they finally got the lamp to work properly.

There is an interesting story by Franklin Y. Fitch in his book, *The Life, Travels and Adventures of an American Wanderer*, (1883) regarding Kennedy.

"Alonzo Pierre Demilt, born in New York City on September 3, 1831, as a very young boy, relocated with his parents, a younger sister, Frances, and infant sister, Elizabeth, to the new town of Port Leon, Florida, in 1839. During the second year of the Demilts' residency there, the town was scourged by a terrible yellow fever epidemic. Alonzo's parents...were stricken and soon died. ...his young sister, Frances, also died. This left Alonzo and his little sister, Elizabeth,...orphans.

"A Mr. Densmore owned ...a tavern across the street from the Demilt home, and he volunteered to take in the young Alonzo Demilt. Densmore treated the boy well for a time, but began to use him as a bar keeper, laborer and errand runner for the bar. Elizabeth, in the meantime, was being well cared for by the widow, Mrs. Spencer, of Port Leon.

"In the course of his stay at the tavern, Alonzo formed the acquaintance of a sturdy, kind-hearted pilot, David Kennedy, who at the time was working at the lighthouse at St. Marks...A confidential friendship was established between Kennedy and Alonzo, and Alonzo communicated to his friend his strong desire to leave.

"[David Kennedy] proposed that young Alonzo accompany him to the lighthouse, and allow Alonzo to make his home there where he would find good friends and kind treatment. Alonzo accepted...A plan was made by Kennedy to secret the boy away on his boat, knowing that Densmore would never give his consent....The plan was successfully carried out. Alonzo slipped away from Densmore, boarded Kennedy's boat, secreted himself behind some old cordage and sails and was soon outward bound to the St. Marks Lighthouse. He was warmly received by the keeper's wife and children...Alonzo got along very well at the lighthouse, where he made his home for some weeks, but was still fearful and longed to return to the security of his relatives in New York. He eventually left the lighthouse by sneaking away and thus began his world wide travels and adventures. In later life, after many years of travels all around the world, Alonzo Demilt settled into his home in Tallahassee, never forgetting the kindnesses of David Kennedy at the St. Marks Lighthouse so many years before."(Fitch, 6-8)

The story is confirmed by Ina Mae Roberts Boykin of Tallahassee. Ina Mae and her family are from Wakulla County and are direct descendants of Kennedy. According to her, the story has been passed down in the family through the years.

(NOTE:) In referring to Kennedy as a "pilot", before he was Keeper at the Lighthouse, he was engaged with other pilots in taking "lighters" from Spanish Hole out in front of the lighthouse up-river to St. Marks, New Port, Port Leon, or Magnolia. "Spanish Hole" was the name given to an area near the mouth of the St. Marks River where the water is deep enough for the anchorage of deep draft ships. "Lighters" were smaller, shallow draft vessels that would take on cargo from the big ships at anchor in Spanish Hole.

In 1880; James H. Breen took over as Keeper, followed by George N. Gibson (1881-1892).

September 9, 1882, George Gibson, Keeper, "Sunset, exhibited light. Storming very hard, wind ENE to S. At 2AM storm abating, dwelling porch and outbuildings washed away…at sunrise…fresh gale wind."

September 30, 1882, Gibson, Keeper, "…Assistant J. Dent relieved from duty by the abolishing of the grade of assistant keeper at the station…"

(NOTE): Prior to this date, the Keeper and his family shared the two bedroom house with the assistant keeper and his family.

October 24, 1882, Gibson, Keeper, "…workmen finished repairs to building and left for New Orleans."

June 30, 1886, Gibson, Keeper, "Watching hurricane."

September 8, 1888, Gibson, Keeper, "Appeared strong storm approaching with winds from the E and barometer falling. 10 boats anchored in Spanish Hole went up river for safety of St. Marks. Storm was not too bad and passed."

June 4, 1890, Gibson, Keeper, "6:30AM, tender Arbutus left for Pensacola."

January 31, 1891, Gibson, Keeper, "Many vessels off sponging…"

June 18, 1891, Gibson, Keeper, "My family returned from Key West…"

November 15, 1891, Gibson, Keeper, "Moon in eclipse… Moon was in eclipse at sunset and remained so until 7:55 being a total eclipse."

January 16, 1892, Gibson, Keeper "Weather very cold, heaviest frost has been here in ten years."

George Gibson continued as keeper until 1892, when Great Grandfather Charles Fine, became the keeper of the St. Marks lighthouse.

St. Marks Lighthouse, circa 1895.

Chapter 3
<u>THE FINES</u>

Charles O. Fine, Sara Jane Fine, and Family.

Our Great Grandfather, Charles Oliver Fine, was born in Key West, Florida, June 20, 1853. Both his parents were born in England. Our Great Grandmother, Sarah Jane Sweeting Fine, was born in Key West in 1856. Her parents, Samuel Sweeting (1830-1914) and Adeline Adams Sweeting (1835-?), were both born in the Bahamas. Prior to 1892, Great Grandpa had been a shoemaker in Key West. His health was poor and he felt that working outdoors would be helpful, and so he went to work with the Light House Service at the Dry Tortugas Lighthouse near Key West. Meanwhile, Gibson's wife, who was also from Key West, became homesick and Gibson requested that Great Grandpa trade lighthouses, and he agreed.

The 1900 census reports Charles as being 47 and Sarah 44 at the time of their residence at the lighthouse in Wakulla County. Their children were Ralph, Horace, Nellie, Linnie, Jennie. Lela (our Grandmother was born January 29, 1893. She was the first of two children born at the lighthouse.). Annie was born in 1895.

Sarah Jane Fine.

(NOTE): John is a member of the Wakulla County Historical Society and often gives talks about life at the lighthouse. I quote him as follows:

"When I give my talks to the historical folks in Wakulla County, I tell them I know that each and every one of them who love Wakulla County either came themselves as recent residents, or many can go back in history and find the person who should be thanked for moving them there. Then I tell them that I can not only do that, but I can tell the exact date, time, and weather conditions when my ancestors arrived in Wakulla County. I can do that because I have found Keeper Gibson's lighthouse log entries in that regard at the National Archives in Washington, D. C. My family has Charles Fine, my great grandfather, to thank, and here are details from the log":

June 30, 1892: Gibson, Keeper, "PM Mr. Charles Fine arrived at station to relieve me. Sunset, exhibited light, moderate breeze south, clear and dry."

July 1, 1892: Gibson, Keeper, "Mr. Fine relieves me today,

St. Marks Lighthouse, circa 1918.

March 7· 1895, Fine, Keeper, "Warf [sic] and boat house, put up one cistern, piazza, new fence, privy repaird. [sic] The station in general fished [sic] work on May 28, 1895 and proceeded to Cedar Key"

December 8, 1900, Inspectors entry, Fine, Keeper, "Inspected station in good condition, except wharf, fence and some shingles on roof—Journal not written in since November 7, 1900. Keeper's left hand disabled."

(NOTE:) According to John, Fine seemed to be a very poor keeper of his logs. He almost never reported anything but weather, and the exhibiting and extinquishing of the light. It appears he would not make his entries and then all at once would sit down and make up his entries. He almost never entered anything of interest, and his handwriting was poor at first and became increasingly so, probably because of ill health.

June 18, 1904, Sarah J. Fine made her first entry as "Keeper".

During Great Grandpa Fine's tenure, Aunt Linnie recalled "…a boat hauling rosin named the 'L.H. Hill' going to Carabelle with its cargo. It always tooted on its way past the light. The engineer on the 'L.H. Hill' would often stop by the lighthouse to play his guitar for her parents and they would waltz together to the delight of their children…"(*Magnolia Monthly*, Vol. II, No. 12)

Great Grandpa Fine died suddenly of what was then called "dropsy of the heart" on August 26, 1905. The next day Sarah continued keeping the logs and took over as the lighthouse keeper. She did not mention his death. Her notes were also about the weather. She continued as keeper until February 28, 1916.

After Great Grandma Fine retired from the lighthouse service and returned to Key West, she was followed by Jesse H. Bishop, a temporary keeper on March 1, 1916, and U.M. Gunn on April 1, 1916. John found that Mr. Gunn kept meticulous records and recorded all of his chores. "Everyday this man did something—not a lazy fellow at all."

Chapter 4
<u>THE GRESHAMS</u>

Our Grandfather, John Young Gresham, was born October 4, 1888, in Fort White, Florida, to Charles and Laura Cone Gresham. His mother died when he was very young, and his father became a wanderer, picking up odd jobs as he moved from one small town to another. He took Young with him, and since there were no child labor laws back then, Young was working by the time he was ten years old in sawmills, or wherever he and his dad could find work.

Lela Fine Gresham, circa 1909.   *John Young Gresham, circa 1909.*

When Young was in his late teens he and his father found work in a pencil factory in Cedar Key, Florida. It was there that he became acquainted with one of the Fine boys, whether it was Ralph or Horace is not known, but he was invited for a visit to the lighthouse. As the story goes, Young was taking a tour and was standing at the rail around the housing at the top of the tower when he looked down to see a young girl looking up at him. The girl was Lela and it wasn't long before Young was courting her. They were married in April of 1909 when Young was 20 and Lela was 16.

Our grandparents, Young and Lela, settled in St. Marks next door to Grandmother's sister and brother-in-law, Linnie and Ernest Oliver. (Lela and Linnie were the only two of the Fine children to stay in St. Marks.) Linnie and Ernest were eventually to have nine children, all of them settling in the area, with the exception of Annie Mary, who settled in Perry, Florida. They were Fred, L.E., Robert, Elmer, Doris, Pearl, Annie Mary, Bond and Myrtle.

Ernest Oliver was a direct descendant of James Llewellyn Oliver (1842-1908), who fought at the Battle of Natural Bridge. (*Magnolia Monthly*, Vol. II, No. 12)

In those days, according to Aunt Linnie,

"The hotels in St. Marks in the early part of the century were numerous, and declined in proportion to the loss in water traffic. But Linnie remembers a two-story wooden hotel next to her house that was a scene of much revelry right after World War I. It was first owned by a man named Duval, then another named Bob Hudson. Men on excursion or in from the boats would stop by for a drink or overnite [sic], and on the upstairs floor they would often be sick vomiting out of the window…Complaints didn't do any good because there were no policemen in St. Marks and the sheriff was too far away, in Crawfordville.

"The Sunday train on the St. Marks Railroad would bring people down from Tallahassee and south Georgia for an excursion. The trip was the important thing, for after they arrived they had time only for a meal in one of St. Marks' hotels, then they'd

John Young and Lela Gresham with first three children, left to right, Vera, Eula, and Alton, circa 1913.

John Young Gresham in U.S. Lighthouse Service uniform, circa 1918.

board the train for the trip home." (*Magnolia Monthly*, Vol. II, No. 12)

Granddaddy went to work for the railroad, and it was during this time that Grandmother gave birth to Eula, January 27, 1910; Alton, August 6, 1912; Vera (our mother), October 14, 1913, and John Young, Jr., or J.Y., on January 16, 1916.

Lela Fine Gresham, circa 1918.

According to Mother, malaria was a problem back then in St. Marks, and the children were sick so often that when Granddaddy heard of an opening at the lighthouse at Cape San Blas near Port St. Joe, Florida, he applied for the job as Assistant Keeper. They were there for only two years when the family moved to the St. Marks Lighthouse where Granddaddy took charge as Keeper, replacing Mr. Gunn.

May 1, 1918, Gunn, Keeper "J.Y. Gresham assumed duties as keeper."

Our family went on to serve as keepers of the St. Marks Lighthouse for a total of 57 years. On an individual basis the fam-

The Gresham family, left to right, Alton, Lela, Vera, Eula, and Young, circa 1919. John Young Gresham, Jr. (J.Y.) is absent from picture.

ily keepers were as follows: Charles Fine: 1892-1904; his wife, Sarah Fine: 1904-1916; their daughter and son-in-law, John Young Gresham and Lela Fine Gresham: 1918-1949; their son, Alton T. Gresham: 1950-1952.

Granddaddy, John Young Gresham, was to serve as the light-house keeper longer than any of the others—a total of 31 years.

Chapter 5
<u>THE HOUSE</u>

When the four Gresham children arrived at the lighthouse one of the first things they noticed was how calm the waters were. They had come from Cape San Blas which was located on a spit that jutted out into deep waters of the Gulf, so that during storms the surf could be formidable. Here on the Apalachee Bay there was only the gentle lapping of the tiny waves upon the shore where the shore birds pecked away for their food and little Fiddler crabs scurried about. Although their first glimpse of the St. Marks light was probably impressive, their living quarters would be far inferior to those at Cape San Blas. The house there was a comfortable two-story structure, wherein the St. Marks living quarters was attached to the tower and only consisted of four rooms with an outhouse. It was primarily accessible by water, making it relatively remote.

From left to right Laura, Edna, Dorothy and Marion (Teebee), circa 1928.

In the subsequent years, four more children were added to the Gresham household: Laura, born May 7, 1921; Edna, born September 25, 1922; Dorothy, born March 17, 1924, and Marion, (known as "Teebee" in the family), born February 12, 1926.

From left to right Marion, Dorothy, Edna, Laura, J.Y., Vera, Lela, and Young, circa 1930.

Many have wondered how a family of ten could have occupied such a small space. In those days many people had large families and small houses, so it was not unusual for several children to share the same bed. As previously noted in the logs of September 30, 1882, Assistant Keeper, Dent, was relieved from duty. Obviously, there had at one time been two families sharing the four-room house.

To give some perspective, I will describe the interior of the house as I remember it during the 1940's. I have also gleaned information from Mother over the years, and more recently from Edna and Dorothy, our aunts.

The lighthouse faces west with the Gulf on the left, primarily, and the road approaching from the north. Across the front was a porch set eight feet above the ground and, at that time, ran the length of the house. The height of the porch offered some protection from storm surges, depending upon the size of the hurricane. Later, a bathroom would be added in the middle of the porch which would cut the porch in half. The walls were four feet thick and heavy doors covered the entrance to the living room on one end of the porch and the kitchen at the other end. During hurricanes the heavy shutters at all the windows were closed. The door to the kitchen was most frequented by friends and family, as that was the gathering place. There was a little sitting area in one corner, while a large round table dominated the center of the room. The appliances lined the walls, with a sink against the back wall and a stove against the north wall. There was also a window on the north wall where Grandmother kept her sewing machine. There were two windows on each side of the kitchen sink with a view of the sand flats and marshy ponds filled with alligators and frequented by beautiful wading birds. The opposite window next to the sitting area looked out onto the porch.

Across the porch from the kitchen was a room which was used for storage primarily, but it was also in this room that Alton and J.Y. slept at times. At other times it was used for the live-in teachers.

There was a hallway running west off the kitchen with two windows overlooking the front porch and the water beyond. All the windows had window seats and were deep enough for me to make playhouses out of them, or simply to curl up with a good book. On the left of the hallway were two bedrooms. The smaller one next to the kitchen was where the girls slept. It had one window facing east and two beds, one on each side of the window. They slept three to a bed. Although this sounds uncomfortable, there was such an age difference from Eula and Marion that Eula left home when Marion was still quite small. I also know that Marion slept with Grandmother when she was a baby. The larger bedroom off the hall and next to the living room was our grandparents' room. It was large enough to accommodate a small bed down at one end next to the fireplace. I suspect that the smallest of the children might have slept there at times. I remember being put down for naps in that bed. There were two windows in that room also overlooking the sand flats.

The St. Marks Lighthouse, circa mid to late 1930s.

At the end of the hall next to the tower was the living room. Just to the right between the tower room and the front door was a small room used for storage. Later it became Granddaddy's office. The living room had two windows overlooking the flats. It was furnished in a deep green wooly-like material, which I thought strange for such a hot climate. The walls were decorated with photographs ordered by Granddaddy from the *National Geographic Magazine*. They were all black and white. A large one over the sofa was of the Matterhorn in Switzerland. Another large one on the tower side of the wall was of a large ship, and there was a small picture of a Bedouin and his camel on the opposite wall. Between the couch and the tower wall was the radio, a center of information vital to Granddaddy's belief of instruction and connection to the outside world. There were several chairs in matching green and floral prints, as well as a piano that sat on the opposite wall from the tower. There was a wood-burning stove on the same wall with the piano and beside the front door, a table with a mirror above it.

Adjacent to the living room was a door leading into the tower room. Spiraling from the center was the staircase attached at one end to a huge post and, at the other end, attached to the wall where there was a handrail made of rope. The structure that included the stairs and post were made of wood. The stairs were wider next to the wall and narrowed closer to the pole. Sometimes I would climb to the first turn and see how close I could get to the pole. (Mother would have had heart failure had she known!) Beneath the bottom of the stairs was a space large enough for a bed and dresser with a mirror. It was here that some of the teachers slept and, at times, Alton and J.Y. A black curtain could be pulled across the opening under the tower for privacy and to shut out the light from the tower. It was surprisingly roomy. It was also eerie in a passive way—the mirror reflecting the tower walls with a hint of disquiet. Everything was covered with battleship gray which gave off an acrid odor, probably from the lead in the paint. Along the walls Granddaddy kept his spyglass, charts and log books. I loved the quiet mystery of this room. It was fun to stand at the foot of the stairs and yell, listening to my voice echo several times from above. I often wondered how anyone could have slept there, as many times the wind would howl through those chambers at night.

At the north end of the front porch, there was what we called a "run" or a continuation of the porch running north. At the end of this extension was the outhouse. It was a two-seater and great at night for watching the light from the tower blink on and off while answering nature's call. My Aunt Marion—or "Teebee", as we called her, would usually accompany me and sit on the lid next to me. It would have been spooky otherwise, as it was quite dark. After the addition of the bathroom, the "run" was taken away. I was not happy about it, as it had been more like a porch with benches for viewing the sunsets, or watching the weather change.

Next to the run near the porch was where rainwater was collected in a large water tank. The "run" had a picket fence on each side and at the water tank the children kept glasses upside down on the pickets. The story goes that Uncle J.Y. went out one night for a glass of water and, after filling his glass from the water tank spigot, swallowed a frog.

Chapter 6
PARADISE

Beyond the house lay a wonderland to explore. When the tide was out the children could wade out to the sand bars—some a half-mile wide. They would hunt for flounders buried just under the sand and all the crabs they could eat. The sand bars were sometimes referred to as oyster bars because they were often covered with oysters. The children would gather those, too.

Across the sand flats behind the lighthouse were a mass of low-lying trees. These were actually two islands—Whale Island and Mini Island. Whale Island got its name from a whale that had washed up there and died sometime in the 1800s. Grandmother told the story of how men from St. Marks went out there and boiled very fine oil from the whale. She said they were able to boil off a number of barrels of oil.

Young Gresham, circa early 40's.

Although the oil had been obtained years before her birth, such a quantity was stored at the lighthouse that they used it for their lamps, including the tower, throughout her youth.

The girls would sometimes accompany Uncle J.Y. on his sailboat to the islands to gather wild pears and swamp cabbage. Sometimes Edna and Teebee would row to the islands on expeditions of adventure.

There was also a beach behind the lighthouse where I remember

Myrna Roberts, circa 1942.

41

going to swim with my aunts. I would also accompany Dorothy and Teebee along the beach as they searched for flounder.

It was a fabulous playground, especially when my cousins, Joann and Sonny, were there. There were even a few hills to run up and down; though rolling down the hill in the sand spurs would have to be one of my less pleasant memories.

There was a garage just north of the fence where Granddaddy kept his jeep, and a small room towards the back of the garage where he kept supplies.

Sometimes Granddaddy would take me on his rounds with him, giving me rides in the wheelbarrow and sitting me on his shoulders as he walked around the ponds looking for wildlife. I remember once going with him in his jeep to see an alligator's nest.

Vera Gresham standing on the old boathouse dock, 1935.

The lighthouse faces west, southwest. Granddaddy had a boathouse about a 100 yards west along a dirt road that ran parallel to the water. This road continued on to Countryman's Hill. It was an unusual hill when the Gresham's first arrived and was named after Mr. Countryman, the elderly gentleman who lived there. As the story goes, Countryman, who lived alone, was wading in the shallow water near his house when he stepped on a stingray. It struck him on the leg, and, lacking proper medical attention, his leg became infected and Mr. Countryman died. Our mother remembered taking food to him. She said he refused any medical assistance, apparently not realizing the seriousness of his condition.

By the time that John and I came along, the old boathouse was still there with only remnants of the dock where seabirds roosted. It was picturesque, but unusable. Sometime after Countryman's demise, a canal was built where the hill had been. It parallels the road and can be accessed about a mile north of the lighthouse. This is where the new boathouse was built. Fishermen launch their boats there now.

As for "Countryman's Hill", John and I had no personal knowledge of Mr. Countryman, and the area next to the canal is now flat with rocks extending out into the bay. According to John, Granddaddy told him "that when they were digging the canal, they destroyed Countryman's Hill, and he observed the hill had logs beneath

Photo of old boathouse dock with lighthouse in view, circa 1935.

the sand of the hill which formed its foundation. Granddaddy said he thought it had to have been the ruins of Fort Williams, a Confederate shore battery. No one has been able to locate the fort, and this could possibly be evidence of its location."

Granddaddy built a white picket fence that surrounded the grounds. Besides the grand old Oak tree in the center of the yard,

Vera Gresham in front of the fig trees, 1935.

there were several palms and cedar trees. He surrounded the Palms with large conch shells and planted Fig trees across the front along the porch. When the figs ripened, he would harvest buckets full of the delicious fruit. How he managed to save them from the raccoons is a mystery. Along the back of the house he planted peach trees that put forth beautiful fruit, also. People are astonished that he was able to grow peaches in that sandy soil, but not only did they thrive, but long after he was gone there were a few still growing there. I remember as a child sitting in a window seat looking down at the peach trees. They were rosy with ripe fruit. Underneath the trees I could also see a large rattlesnake making its way through the grass—paradise, snake and all.

Vera Gresham at the lighthouse. Brick walk was later replaced by concrete.

Chapter 7
<u>DAILY BREAD/DAILY CHORES</u>

In the early years, Granddaddy would fish at night to supplement the family larder. He also had a vegetable garden and a cucumber vine along the fence that he had to cut down, as it grew too large for the fence. At various times, the family had a cow (which did not survive one of the hurricanes), pigs, and chickens. The cow had become something of a pet to the children, and they mourned her death. The pig, unfortunately, was also a pet named "Ernie", and when Granddaddy slaughtered it for dinner, the children stood around the table and cried. Thus, "Ernie" was given a proper burial, and that was the end of raising livestock.

In addition to the problem of dining on the family "pets", there were many hurricanes during those days, and the high water not only killed the animals and chickens, but would drown the garden. So Granddaddy finally had to rely on fishing and the market. Once a week he would take his small 20-foot launch into St. Marks to pick up the mail and a weekly supply of groceries. He would always buy candy for the children.

The Greshams had plenty of food during the Great Depression. Granddaddy would order supplies from Jacksonville that would be sent by train to St. Marks. These were mostly staples, such as peas, corn, tomatoes, okra, beets and beans. There were huge jars of raisins, prunes, canned peaches and pears. There were also huge sacks of dried beans, Irish potatoes, sweet potatoes, and onions. Because there was no refrigeration, they would order Pet milk and dilute it with water. There was also plenty of rice, grits, flour, and meal. They had marsh hens and fish for meat; corned beef hash, corned beef, white side meat, and pork in kegs of briney water. They would boil the salt off and cook it with vegetables or beans. There was also syrup, and they got their butter in St. Marks. Eventually, the family received a gas refrigerator. Mother remembers how wonderful it was to have cold milk. They would make sweet drinks by adding chocolate, vanilla or fruit—a real treat in such a hot climate.

Among his many talents, Granddaddy also enjoyed cooking, and he had some specialties. I remember the perfect cup of cocoa that he would make just for me. He would allow me to pour it into my saucer to cool, so I wouldn't burn my lip. I've never been able to duplicate that wonderful cocoa flavor the way he made it. He also created a recipe for sweet muffins, which he called "Granddaddy's Specials" and indeed they were. Sometimes he would cut the heart out of the Cabbage Palm and cook it. He called it "palmetto cabbage." Aunt Edna recently wrote an article for the Tallahassee *Democrat*, and I quote her:

Every Christmas my father would build a small fire in order to cook the cabbage in a large black cast-iron pot, seasoning it with ham or salt pork. Along with this we ate a pan of cornbread, sweet potatoes, lima beans, and fried mullet.

Granddaddy would sometimes cook up a batch of the palmetto cabbage for John and me. It was quite good, much like regular cabbage with a slightly bitter taste.

So the family ate well—plain fare, but nutritious. These comestibles had to feed a family of ten and usually two or three men who would be working on the grounds or painting and, part of the year, a live-in school teacher. There were also unexpected visitors.

Mr. Sawyer, Lighthouse inspector.

Log Entry, March 5, 1932: "Strong wind from SE, rain. *Miss New Port* blown ashore and holes torn in bottom by beating against the wharf. Several boards were knocked off the wharf. The party of six remained at station all night."

Log Entry, June 3, 1932: "A Mr. Grantham and two sons of Fanlew, Florida, were given two meals each and lodging. Mr. Kreager visited station." (Paul Kreager was the first manager of the St. Marks Wildlife Refuge.)

How they managed sleeping accommodations for these visitors is a mystery. I would assume they spent the night in the room across the porch.

The care and maintenance of a lighthouse is much like a ship. The exterior of the house and tower constantly exposed to the harsh environment of heat, humidity, salt and sunlight, required gallons of white paint and battleship gray. All the walls were white, except for the outside steps, the porch and the tower steps. These were battleship gray. I believe the shutters and doors were also trimmed with the blue-gray. Besides the buildings, the white picket fence also required maintenance. Granddaddy always hired professionals to paint the tower including most of the other exteriors. The boys, Uncles Alton and J.Y., helped Granddaddy with some of the heavy chores. One of their responsibilities was to scrub the steps outside as well as the tower steps—not an enviable task. However, since both Alton and J.Y. left home to join the Coast Guard when they were 16 years old, Granddaddy had to rely heavily on outside help. He would hire local men to help him do odd jobs around the grounds, and that included some painting of the outbuildings, and the interior. There is frequent mention of "Henry". He mowed the grass and trimmed trees.

John, in his research of the logbooks, discovered that Grand-daddy was meticulous. He was also a very busy man and daily entries report the assorted work he did, from polishing the lens, sweeping the stairs, painting, building and general maintenance repair work. The grounds, including the enclosing white picket fence, were perfectly maintained.

In Log entry, July 10, 1937, he opines "I wonder if anyone really knows just how much a Keeper puts in each day on duty." Evidently, the logs sometimes doubled as a journal.

John noted besides the constant painting, planting, and trimming his shrubs and trees, scrubbing, build-

John Young Gresham, circa early 1930s.

47

ing all kinds of things from window frames to ladders, visiting his aids to navigation out in the river (buoys and beacons), Granddaddy made numerous trips by boat to St. Marks to pick up mail, buy supplies, and take people to and from the train station. He was constantly having to rescue boats of all sizes grounded on the numerous oyster and sand bars out in the Bay. About every other year a hurricane would blow through, which meant more clean-up, repair and rebuilding.

Batteries were used to light the beacons that marked the channel. Changing the batteries on the beacons was a difficult and even dangerous job. They had to be charged frequently and repairs were constant. The front beacon, and the most important, was especially problematic. It would flash erratically, burn steady or go out. The beacons had timers on them to regulate the on and off blinking intervals. Quite often the problem was bird poo or salt intrusion into the workings of the flasher. Grandaddy or one of the children would check that light each night from the tower, as it was a critical one to begin to guide vessels into the river channel after dark.

Log entry Sep. 19, 1931, "Went to St.Marks for beacon material, *USLHS Aster* and *Magnolia* arrived 10:30 am to build beacons"

Mother wrote a column for the *Wakulla County News*. In one of her columns she remarks on the gasoline business and comments on the inadequacy of the channel.

GASOLINE BUSINESS IN ST. MARKS; NEWPORT
(By Vera Gresham)

"Judging from what I see from the lighthouse, the gasoline business in St. Marks and Newport is evidently growing.

"Within the past ten days the *Gulf Spray* has made three trips up the river, and the *Carmelina*, one trip. I have been informed correctly this means that about 390,000 gallons of gasoline has been stored in tanks at St. Marks and Newport.

Dredging Boat, St. Marks River.

"The *Gulf Spray* is a small, steel tanker that comes from Port Tampa, Fla. It is owned by the Gulf Refining Co., and brings to St. Marks about 130,000 gallons of gasoline each trip. The *Carmelina* is a small tug boat that tows a steel barge from Mobile, Ala., to Newport for the Citizen's Oil Co. The capacity of the barge is about the same as that of the *Gulf Spray*.

"The *Gulf Spray* finds it difficult in getting to St. Marks because of a crooked and shallow channel. It is rumored that the channel will be straightened and deepened from the Gulf to Newport some time in the near future. We have no assurance of this, however; we only hope it is true."

Apparently they did begin dredging the channel in 1933.

Log entry, Nov. 20, 1933 "…Stanbury's dredge arrived to start work…Keeper assisted and worked with dredge crew."

During the early fall, dog flies were a big problem.

Dredge boat crew.

Log entry, September 29, 1937, "Worked on wheel barrow, scrubbed floors and primarily fought dog flies…" and again on September 14, 1940, "Light NE wind with a billion dog flies."

There is proof that political correctness existed even back in Granddaddy's day—or, perhaps Granddaddy invented it. Periodically in his logs he refers to a rock on the east flats as "Negro Head Rock". It was locally known as "Nigger Head Rock", not in a mean-spirited way, but due to common usage during those days. Granddaddy seemed to realize that it was not proper and was more gentlemanly in his reference to it.

Also, proof that Granddaddy was an honest man is reflected in his log entry on August 19, 1939: "I am afraid that I passed a small skiff aground on bar that I should have stopped and asked the persons if they needed assistance." Since the logs were regularly inspected by the lighthouse service agents, he could have easily omitted this observation.

Granddaddy sometimes had to "police" the area, as in the log entry of June 5, 1932, "Refused to allow four picnickers to spread dinner on station wharf."

But on September, 10, 1936, he was more amenable, "… two old folks allowed to camp on beach overnight."

There were some entries that were puzzling, this one from Mother, "June 12, 1932: Mr. Shields of St. Marks brought a party of four and requested me to allow them a short visit to the station. I refused."

Mr. Shields was an entrepreneur in St. Marks. In fact, he

eventually leased the river front property to Daddy for his business. There was no reason given for this denial, but I will hazard a guess. Many years ago Mother told me that Mr. Shields, who could be quite devilish, would sometimes go goose hunting on the Refuge during the off season and then invite Paul Kreager, the Refuge Manager, for dinner!

Here are a few more log entries which gives us a daily picture of the Lighthouse Keeper's routine.

Log Entry, Feb. 11, 1933 "Gave 3 men supper and room for night. Names of men: Jesse Porter, Ed Nickles, and Charles Crumb."

Log Entry, Mar. 12, 1933 "Gave Bud Strickland and Jim Barker, fishermen, 3 gals.gasoline." (NOTE) Providing gasoline to those in need was a regular event.

Log Entry, Sep. 14, 1933 "Went to St. Marks on leave; wife in charge of station."

Log Entry, Aug. 31, 1937 "40-50 mile gale from south. Tanker *Gulf Spray* came in during worst part of gale. Barometer lowest, 29.88. Rain most of day. (NOTE): In those days the only indication of an approaching hurricane was barometer readings. This one would have been suspicious.

Log Entry, Jan. 16, 1937 "Ten-

The Camellia.

der *Camellia* delivered supplies to station, arriving at 4pm left at 1030am next day." (Note: Alton

The Camellia *crew. Uncle Alton is kneeling in front on the right.*

served on the *Camellia* and was probably aboard the boat on this particular day. Alton was a favorite of Dorothy, and I remember her saying how much she looked forward to watching for his boat and visit.)

Log Entry, Sept 24, 1937 "Loaned dinghy to Biological Survey engineer. He left it anchored 300 yards from shore and in an awful mess."

Hunters were frequent visitors. Young is second from left.

Log Entry, Dec. 3, 1937 …"Aaron Brown visited with us till 9:30 waiting for his party of hunters." (NOTE): Granddaddy often entertained hunters at the lighthouse.

A generator was finally installed at the lighthouse, thus providing electricity for the house and tower, a vast improvement, no doubt.

Log entry, May 27, 1939, "Received and stored Delco generators and batteries for this station." (NOTE:) When John and I were very young, the generator was still being used. I remember it was attached to the outside wall of the room across the porch, it was next to the steps, and when we were gathered in the kitchen-dining area, it was quite noisy.

When radios were invented, lighthouses were the first to get them. The family sat with ear phones at first, according to both Mother and Edna. Later, of course, no headsets were necessary.

The pleasures of living at the lighthouse were many, but danger was ever present, and sometimes there were emergencies. The main responsibility of a lighthouse keeper is to rescue boats in distress. Weather on the Gulf is predictable, particularly during the summer when we have daily thunderstorms, or squalls. The beautiful cumulus clouds on the horizon begin to darken as the day wears on and the heat intensifies. This is followed by distant thunder that gradually grows louder, accompanied by lightening. Natives of the area know to watch these daily signs, but anyone unfamiliar with the climate can easily get caught off guard. Though these storms are over quickly, they can also come on suddenly and can be quite violent, sometimes spawning water spouts. Then there was the yearly hurricane season, beginning in July and sometimes reaching into October. So Granddaddy had to keep a close lookout for boats in trouble. He sometimes had to make a dramatic life or death rescue.

The Tallahassee *Daily Democrat*, April 4, 1947
"Lighthouse Keeper Saves 4 Fishermen"
"Keeper J.Y. Gresham, keeper for the past 30 years was starting to get into his auto Sunday morning, heard faint yells from the gulf.[sic] He went out in his motorboat and found 4 men about 2 miles out, clinging to their capsized boat for about an hour. Gresham could hear them because of a stiff breeze blowing in to shore. The men were from Albany, Ga. Gresham only got one name, B.J. Dickenson."

Eula Gresham, circa 1928.

All in a day's work—run some errands, do some maintenance work; save a few lives.

Grandmother and the two oldest girls, Aunt Eula and Mother, also had plenty of work. Grandmother was an excellent seamstress and spent almost all her waking hours making clothes for the children. They probably ordered most of the boy's clothes from Sears and Roebuck, but she sewed the girls' clothes, and with six girls one can only imagine the time spent at the sewing machine. Because this was such a time-consuming job, she needed help with the other responsibilities. While Eula was home, she was the "chief cook and bottlewasher." The four younger girls, Laura, Edna, Dorothy and Teebee, were under Mother's care. This was a perfect balance, as Eula was efficient, but not so patient as Mother,

From left to right back row, Young, Lela, Eula, Vera, J.Y. Front row from left, Marion, Edna, and Dorothy, circa 1928.

54

so that Mother became something of a "surrogate mother" to the four little girls.

Unfortunately, for Mother, Aunt Eula was headstrong and defied Granddaddy by eloping with a local boy who had been hired to help Granddaddy with some painting. Granddaddy disowned her (temporarily) and Mother had to take over Eula's chores. She did so cheerfully and, with Grandmother, was able to help take on household maintenance, especially the cooking. She not only managed Eula's responsibilities as well as her own with the children, but found time to write a column for the Wakulla *County News* and kept up a correspondence with pen pals around the world.

Being closest to Mother, of course, I had listened to the longing in her voice as she told me of her early childhood at Cape San Blas and at St. Marks when she could still go out and play. She remembered going out on the sand flats in St. Marks and sitting on the bow of a skiff, letting her feet dangle in the cool water. She told me about a special doll, named "Julie" she had in Cape San Blas. She had been playing with her on the beach when she was called inside. Sadly, she left her doll behind, and a storm came up during the night and washed her away. It was a sad story that she always remembered. When Mother was only eight years old, she was handed her infant sister, Laura, to help care for. From then on, my mother lost much more than her doll. She lost her childhood.

Chapter 8
<u>THE CHILDREN</u>

According to Aunt Edna the four younger girls got off lightly. During my work on this book, she sent me a letter detailing some of her memories.

"When I was small I was assigned the 'job' of feeding the chickens. One day when I was going down the steps with the feed, a giant rattlesnake was crawling under the steps. I screamed and dropped all of the feed. J.Y. shot him dead and hung him on a tree.

Edna Gresham, circa 1928.

"During the winter school days, we were responsible for our clothes. We had to wash, starch and iron our clothes on weekends. Of course, we did this all year long."

However, she goes on to say

"We girls spent hours rocking and singing songs on the front porch. We had large white rocking chairs and used them often. Papa was supposed to be a very strict man, but he made us lazy as he did not assign us much of anything to do."

Edna has fond memories of Mother, as well as her other sisters.

"Vera took care of we four younger girls. She bathed us, washed our hair; read to us, and many other caring things.

She was everything to me, and I could write a book on the numerous and endless, wonderful things she did. When she left home I cried for days. We continued to be close even after she married. She was a great lady, and I shall never forget her.

"Laura could play the piano which made you want to sing and clap your hands. The fishermen would slowly row their

boats past the house while she was 'beating' out a tune. She was talented and smart, but rather shy, which held her back in many things. She was an "A" student in high school.

"Dorothy was brilliant and wanted perfection! She was an A+ student and graduated from Crawfordville High School as Valdictorian.."

Edna describes Marion as sweet and gentle and Eula as a bit

Laura Gresham, circa 1937.

vain, or as being careful with her appearance. I remember that Eula had beautiful hair, which was honey-colored like Grandmother's.

Edna goes on to describe herself as "a happy-go-lucky girl who enjoyed having fun. In the summer I spent hours playing on the beach, rounding up fiddlers, collecting arrowheads and shells, swimming every day, and reading the *National Geographic Magazine.* I gigged flounders in the

Edna Gresham, circa 1940.

Eula and Roy Donaldson, circa 1940.

evening. I was a good student when I liked the subject, but if I did not like the subject I would almost fail, particularly algebra!"

Business was evidently Aunt Edna's strong point. She attended Lively Technical Institute, which served her well later in life as a business woman. She later married Dallas Lambert, a building contractor. He gave Edna the rental business he owned, and she became responsible for its maintenance. She and Dallas had one son, Dallas, Jr., who has continued in his father's footsteps, as a successful builder.

Edna lived with us in St. Marks when she first left home. She went to work for Citizens Oil Company. They had holding tanks in St. Marks, which were within walking distance to our house. Was she ever high spirited! My first memory of her was helping Mother with the dishes and singing her heart out!

All these "children" and their families were part of my life, as most of us lived either in Wakulla or Leon County. That would include the Olivers whose children were also my friends and playmates.

By the time I was born, Eula had remarried Roy Donaldson, and they lived in Mobile. They had one son, Stanley. Eula and Roy later settled in Miami and Ft. Pierce ... Eula was predeceased by Roy, and she passed away in September 1995.

Alton, who was close to mother— they were only 14 months apart—was a frequent visitor in our home. He married the former Connie Mann and had two children,

Alton Gresham, circa 1930.

(Left) Joann Gresham, 1958 May Court, Leon High School, Tallahassee.

(Right) Alton Gresham, Jr. (Sonny), circa 1955.

Alton, Jr. (Sonny) and Joann. Sonny and Joann were close in age to John and me, and the four of us were playmates and life-long friends. Sadly, all of them have passed away, with Sonny as the last survivor, in January 2010. He and his wife, Millie, lived in Woodville, Florida. Joann and her husband, Vernon Brown, had settled in Cumming, Georgia.

J.Y. and Helen Gresham, circa 1940.

As for J.Y., he and his family lived in Mobile and we visited them often. I remember him as very funny, if a bit eccentric, with many interesting stories about his days in the Coast Guard. He and his wife, Helen, had four boys, John, Jimmy, Joe and Steve. Their oldest son, John, was about my age, so I always looked forward to visiting them. I remember Uncle J.Y. had an old Model T, which he kept shiny and in such good running condition that he and all his family would drive over to Tallahassee in it. This always embarrassed John to my amusement. J.Y. passed away in January of 1971.

Laura was a wonderful person with a kind heart. She was very intelligent and talented, and could play the piano. Laura married Andrew Pickles from Tallahassee. They had two children, Andy and Donna, and settled in Woodville. I remember she was an excellent cook, so that John and I always looked forward to our visits to Woodville. Another bonus for John and me was that Laura lived next door to "Aunt Pearl", or Pearl and Cajah Vause. Their two children, Ann and Phillip, were good friends, also

Dorothy and Elmo Prater with their children, left to right, Phyllis, Lamar and Carol on Pensacola Street, Tallahassee, Florida, circa 1959.

Dorothy and Teebee were like my older sisters. They stayed with us in Tallahassee after we moved there in 1944. We stayed in Tallahassee during the school terms because of the excellent schools there. Dorothy and Teebee were both attending Florida State College for Women, and for most of that time, they stayed with us until both of them married.

Dorothy was the only one of the Gresham children to graduate from college. She married Elmo Prater, who was the son of W.L. Prater, the Chief of Police in Tallahassee for many years. Dorothy and Elmo had three children, Lamar, who passed away in February 2003; Phyllis and Carol—both married and living in Atlanta. When Lamar, Phyllis and Carol were small, Dorothy and Elmo lived downstairs in the garage apartment of our home on Pensacola Street in Tallahassee. Thus, the children became special to John and me.

Teebee was artistic and very good with children. She spent a lot of time with me and taught me songs. She had a beautiful voice, and her favorite song was *Trade Winds*, a popular Bing Crosby song in the '40s, which she would sing to me. I find it romantic that we both would live in Hawaii. She married Mike Patronis, from Tallahassee, and they lived in Hawaii for many years. I visited them in 1967

where I met my future husband, George, who happened to be working with Mike. Mike and Teebee had two sons, Bill and David.

Marion and Mike Patronis in Hawaii, circa 1954.

Marion (Teebee) Gresham, circa 1948.

Chapter 9
EPISODES FUN, NEAR TRAGIC AND UNIQUE

It was not all work at the lighthouse. The unique environment "out on the point" as the family referred to it, offered many varied experiences. Life was mostly a round of routine interspersed with pleasant

Second from left, Esther Roberts (Wilbur's sister), Vera, Laura, Edna, Dorothy, and Marion. Aunt Esther also taught at the lighthouse. The man is unidentified. Photo, circa 1930.

episodes like the time after a storm surge, some boards or planks washed up on the shore, probably from a ship carrying lumber. Alton and J.Y. dragged the lumber up onto a high place in back of the light and built a little house about 12x12 feet. They installed windows, a door, a nice floor and even a porch. The children would cook in there; sit and talk, enjoying their little house. A hurricane finally carried it back to sea again.

Other times the children would find all sorts of interesting items washed overboard off ships and brought ashore after strong

The four young girls on the ledge surrounding the tower are (from left to right) Marion, Dorothy, Edna, and Laura. Their hair was cropped short for convenience. Photo, circa 1930.

winds and storm surges—items such as tin cups, oars, life preservers and clothing.

Hurricanes

During the years that the Greshams were in residence at the lighthouse, the hurricanes that came ashore were apparently not as dangerous as those earlier ones. Granddaddy still had to rely on the barometer readings, but he also had a radio. Otherwise, he would not have put his family at risk. Thus, the family witnessed many hurricanes. Mother described the noise of the wind like a freight train coming through the house. The winds would always come first from the east, and during this time they could stand out on the porch against the tower wall. The water would roll into the yard so that it looked like the whole Gulf was coming towards them. There would be debris floating around the yard from the destruction of the out-buildings. Snakes would be curled on some of the planks floating in the yard. When Granddaddy was raising animals and chickens, they would drown. After awhile there would be a lull and the sun would come out, and it would be a beautiful day except that the water would be in turmoil, leaping straight up. Then the winds and rain would start to pick up coming from the opposite direction, and

View from the tower after a hurricane.

it would vent its full fury again. Afterward, everything was clear and the weather was perfect. Unfortunately, there was a lot of cleanup. The venerable old Oak tree that still stands in the middle of the yard has taken quite a beating from all the hurricanes.

Aunt Linnie describes a hurricane that hit the lighthouse when she and Grandmother were children:

> One year…a huge tidal wave washed away the boathouse, the fence, and nearly everything else but the tower itself. The family stood up on the steps of the tower during the worst pounding of the waves. When the water subsided they looked out to see that all of their hogs, horses, and mules had been swept away and all of the chickens except those they had managed to bring inside. The front porch, which had been torn off, was swept back and splintered to pieces against the base of the light. The first huge wave had come at night and when it smashed against the tower they thought a ship had hit it…for six months a load of government men, coming in by water, worked to rebuild the barracks and outbuildings surrounding the light.

FUN

Granddaddy was quite strict, as most men of his generation. Grandmother was his opposite, easy-going and fun to be with. Granddaddy required dinner (the noon meal) be on the table at twelve sharp. Eula or Mother usually cooked the meals, but when Granddaddy was away Grandmother would prepare dinner and they might not eat until 2:00 in the afternoon. The children loved the slow pace and my mother remembered how relaxed and happy everyone was at the dinner table when Grandmother was in charge. She would laugh and talk with them—quite a departure from the "being seen but not heard" routine.

> According to Mother, "Alton was the mischievous one, often doing things to tease or frighten the younger ones. The thing he did that stands out most vividly were the times he would go to the top of the tower and go outside where

there is a ledge about three feet wide. There is an iron rail around the ledge and he would climb over the ledge, stand on the outside, hold on with one hand and with one leg extended out in the air, eighty feet up, yell down to us to watch him! We had chickens and I recall once Alton took a hen up to the top of the tower and threw her off to see if chickens could fly. She did."

At other times during Granddaddy's infrequent absences, Alton, Mother and J.Y. would run the flag up to signal the boys out on the boats that they were free to party. Most of the boys were old friends and some of them cousins. They would row ashore and while Mother cooked and baked cookies, the boys would put planks on the outside steps and roll the piano down into the yard. They would then have music with their picnic until their friends would have to row back to their boats.

Two of the boys were Foster Gay and his brother, Maurice. They were from Newport Richie, and were frequent vis-

Maurice Gay, circa 1932.

itors to the lighthouse. They were adventurers who sailed all around the Florida coast and would often anchor off the lighthouse. They became close friends of the Greshams, and I am quite sure that they were among the young men who came ashore to party. I remember Mother telling me that one of them was always singing *I'm Headed for the Last Roundup* as he went about his daily chores on the *Polly*; the song stayed in her memory and always reminded her of her friend. I believe she

Foster Gay, circa 1932.

said that one of them had a crush on her, but for Mother they were both dear, lifelong friends. She told me about one of them, who had settled in Jacksonville, visiting her in Tallahassee when they were both in their declining years. He worked for a citrus packing company in Jacksonville and always sent us a crate of oranges at Christmas. I don't remember which one of the brothers he was, but he outlived Mother. I remember he sent flowers to her funeral.

One of the brothers, and again I'm not sure if it was Foster or Maurice, sent John a copy of his log book. John remembers he wrote about his first trip to the lighthouse and how Granddaddy and one of his daughters—perhaps, Mother—took him up into the tower....

> According to Mother: "Even though my father was very strict, he allowed this, as he also enjoyed the company of others. We would make hot chocolate; sometimes I would bake a cake and the boys would help me. They would bring food from the ship—often fish—and we would cook and have a party with the whole family joining in. I could play the piano and could play only hymns, but that was okay. I would play and they would sing."

There were also many family gatherings in New Port for picnics, as recorded in the Log entry dated June 4, 1941, "Family picnic at New Port". (This has been a favorite picnic area for many generations of Wakulla County residents. It is located beside the St. Marks River across from the turn-off that leads to the lighthouse.)–

> According to Mother, "The only way I ever dated was when the young man left the ship alone; came to the house late in the afternoon or early evening, and we'd sit and talk, play checkers, play records and sometimes work on a jigsaw puzzle. My father never allowed me to leave the house with a young man. That didn't matter, though. I had a dozen proposals of marriage!"

Mother wrote the following letter to Dorothy Dix when she was only 16 years old. It reflected a wisdom which exceeded that of most young girls:

"Dear Miss Dix: When I was 15 years old, I used to have a lot of trouble with my boy friends. They were always getting peeved about something and breaking away and it was hard to get them back. But now I'm a year older and I have thought out a system that works and I give it to other girls free. It is this: Keep yourself neat and attractive and always act as if you are having a wonderful time, no matter whether you are or not. Go out with other boys and have fun. Your heart won't be in it at the begining, but gradually you really will begin to enjoy yourself. Above all, ignore the boy. Don't speak to him. Don't even let him see you looking at him. If he thinks you don't worry about him, he will come back to see why you don't. Don't try to find out whom he has been stepping out with. If you try this plan for one month, I am sure you will get him back. I did. When he is back, you don't throw up other girls to him. Don't let him know you are jealous. Keep him guessing. GOOD LUCK"

Perhaps Mother's wisdom sprung from necessity. Granddaddy was very strict when it came to dating. Obviously, a certain maturity on her part was required to maintain a balance, as illustrated here:

"One thing I recall is if a boy visited me and stayed as late as 10 p.m., my father would have planted an alarm clock in a closet that was in the living room and promptly at 10 it would go off—a signal it was time for that young man to go!

We visited Aunt Linnie, my mother's sister, once a month. "We would go to St. Marks in the launch on Sunday and attend the small church and eat at my aunt's house. We always looked forward to those visits. Often we would plan to go and the wind would blow hard from the south and cause the water to be rough, and our trip would be postponed until another Sunday. I remember how unhappy this would make me. We often went as long as three months in the winter without seeing anyone outside the family. We were never lonely, however. With our large family we were always busy and thoroughly entertained. We didn't know what it was like to have friends and neighbors, so we didn't miss it"

"Once I had a boyfriend. He was 16 and I was 15. His father was a fisherman and took his son along with him when school was out. I'd met him at church in St. Marks and would talk briefly after church. He would write me notes and give them to my cousin to give to me when I was in St. Marks again."

"One day my boyfriend and his father had anchored near the light, so my boyfriend wanted to tell me something and, having no paper or pen, he found a large Irish potato and carefully carved "I love you" on the potato; and a plan to meet; then rowed ashore and stuck it on a stick out back of the house where he knew I'd find it."

"Once I had a letter from a man telling me how much he loved me, but he did not sign his name, only 'Your Phantom Lover', the postmark was St. Marks; the letter was typed, so no way could I know who it was from. There was a letter every Saturday for over a year. To this day, I don't know the writer."

So, for Mother, there is no doubt that "romance" was not just a word to describe flaming sunsets or tropical moons. Romance was an invitation to a tryst written on a potato, or anonymous admirers inspired with poetic devotion.

NEAR-TRAGIC

From left to right, Lela, Aunt Esther, and J.Y., circa 1931.

J.Y. taught himself to sail, and would sometimes take the other children with him to the islands where they would gather wild pears and palmetto cabbage.

J.Y.'s interest in boats and the water was surprising since he had nearly drowned when he was a small child. He and Alton were in the boathouse when J.Y. bumped his head on something and fell into the water. The tide was up and the water was about eight feet deep. Alton started screaming for help. Granddaddy was taking his usual afternoon nap, but luckily Great Grandpa Charles was sitting on the front porch and heard Alton. He ran down to the boathouse and jumped into the water and swam in the direction he assumed J.Y. was drifting. By the grace of God, he found J.Y. immediately. In the meantime all the family had run down to the wharf. J.Y. was pale and was not breathing. Just about that time some fishermen were on their way out to fish beyond the lighthouse when they heard the commotion. They stopped to help and one of the men in the party knew how to give resuscitation. He worked on J.Y. for about thirty minutes, as water kept pouring from his nose and mouth. Finally he yelled "Take me out of this water!" and the whole family wept with relief. After a few days of rest and a trip to the doctor who pronounced him in good condition, he was fine. Besides becoming a self-taught sailor, he later joined the Coast Guard and saw action during World War II, surviving the great typhoon of December 1944, off the coast of Japan. Obviously, his near drowning had no negative long-term affects.

Laura also fell overboard off the dock one day. Alton and J.Y. were watching some fishermen when they suddenly heard a loud splash behind them. One of the boys said "That must have been a big fish. Let's go look!" Then they saw their little three year old sister. She had slipped away from the yard, crawled through a hole that was under the fence and had followed her brothers down to the boathouse. Alton hurriedly slid down a post that supported the dock and rescued her. The water was only about four or five feet deep. There were a lot of barnacles on the post and Alton was quite skinned up from the slide. Laura was fine after coughing and screaming—more frightened than anything.

There were other near tragedies. Mother remembers rescuing another of her small sisters who had fallen into the water. Alton had to hold her ankles as she reached for the child's hair, just barely able to grab her before she slipped away. I'm not sure, but I believe the child was Dorothy. Dorothy also gave them a scare one day as several of the children were out for a stroll. She was jumping up and down on some tall grass overlaying a path, saying what a cushiony pile of grass it was! Horrified, the others could see a rattlesnake coiled beneath her feet. Somehow, Dorothy escaped being bitten. They were all lucky to survive their sometimes very dangerous environment.

UNIQUE

Besides these "everyday" episodes, there were times when the family's unique circumstances invited unique experiences.

The family recalled seeing Halley's Comet pass over the lighthouse in the spring of 1910, a very impressive sight. The lighthouse was a perfect place to view the night sky. Other than the tower and the beacons, there were no other lights to dim the panoramic view of the heavens. Vera remembers being in a skiff one night off shore and seeing a comet hit the water. She remembered it lit up the surrounding area like daylight.

Another time, some of the fishermen off the light swore they saw the Northern lights.

The Dirigible

"Flying Things" were rare sights back in the early 20s, especially in Wakulla County. One day in late August or early

USS Shenandoah *moored at NAS Lakehurst, NJ, circa 1924-1925.*

September 1925, the family at the lighthouse looked up at the sky to discover a huge dirigible silently gliding overhead. It was the Navy dirigible *Shenandoah,* with 43 aboard which was later ripped apart during a thunderstorm on September 3, 1925, splitting into three sections near Caldwell in the southeastern part of Ohio. The storm winds of 70 miles per hour tore loose the airship's control cabin. Lt. Cmdr. Zachary Lansdowne and seven crew members were killed, along with passengers in the tail section. Fourteen men were killed; 29 survived. (Chabek, Lakewood *Sun Post*)

Imagine seeing such a sight and then hearing about its demise so soon afterwards!

Symphonia

The Ringling Brothers' Yacht, the *Symphonia*, anchored off the lighthouse in Spanish Hole on more than one occasion. The children were excited and spent hours looking at it with Granddaddy's powerful telescope. One day the children were invited to come aboard and were served ice cream and cookies. They were taken on a tour of the yacht and Edna describes it as "rich and beautiful."

According to John, Granddaddy took the Ringlings on a goose-hunting trip and allegedly killed a goose, allowing Mrs. Ringling to believe she had shot it. This so pleased the lady, that she later, as a gesture of gratitude, paid Grandmother's hospital bill for an operation on her legs.

The Ringling yacht, the Symphonia.

The Burning of the *Dispatch*

The *Dispatch*, according to Uncle Alton, was used by the Florida Shellfish Commission (no longer a government agency) as a pleasure craft for government personnel. The ship was anchored at Long Bar near the St. Marks Lighthouse in 1928 when an onboa

(Left) Crew of the Symphonia. *Mrs. Ringling is front row on the left.*

On the Symphonia. *Back row from left to right, Mrs. Ringling, Lela, a crew member, J.Y., and front row from left to right, Laura, Marion, Dorothy, and Edna, 1929.*

Mrs. Ringling in the stern of the Symphonia *tender with guests.*

The Symphonia *crew.*

The sinking of the Dispatch *from the old boathouse dock 1928.*

The sinking of the Dispatch 1928.

generator caught fire while running. The ship became engulfed in flames as people were seen diving into the water. Granddaddy responded with his launch and towed the burning yacht away from the channel. He towed it until it ran aground where it finished burning and sank. Before its use by the Shellfish Commission, it had been a private yacht, later donated to the U.S. Navy for use as a sub chaser during World War I. As far as I know, there were no lives lost when it caught fire off the lighthouse. It remained near the channel not far from the mouth of the river for many years.

Crew of the Dispatch *1928.*

Sponge Fishing

Log entry: June 5, 1941, "Counted 9 Greek spongers going into St. Marks."

Mother wrote the following article in one of her columns for the Wakulla *County News* regarding the sponge fishermen.

<u>SPONGE FISHING</u>
(By Vera Gresham)

Greek sponge boat.

"Among the many visitors to the lighthouse this week were several sponge fishermen who came inside because of strong winds. It is interesting to hear them tell of their experiences with sharks twenty feet in length, and of the acres of coral and beautifully colored plants that they see thru their glass-bottom buckets while in search of the little animal—the sponge."

"It is strange but true that the sponge is an animal that lays eggs. The eggs attach themselves to rocks and proceed to grow like plants; they reach marketable size in one year."

Greek sponge boat.

"It is said that more sponge are gathered from Ocklocknee River to Cedar Key than any other area of the same size on earth."

"Supply and demand govern the price of sponge. At present there is a world shortage of the product and the price, which is $8.00 per bunch or $3.50 per pound, is higher than it has been in eight years."

"Clear skies with light breezes, plenty sponge and high prices make all good spongers happy."

Greek Sponge boats operated out of ports like Apalachicola and Tarpon Springs. There are many natives of the Florida panhandle who count the Greeks among their forebears. Many are descendants of those early sponge fishermen. Teebee's husband, Mike Patronis, was of Greek ancestry.

John writes: "There are many commercial grade sponges out on the grass flats in the vicinity of the St. Marks Lighthouse. Because the water on the flats is fairly shallow, maybe 10-15 feet, on average, many of the Tarpon Springs sponge boats would gather on the flats near the lighthouse in the summer months."

"These Greek boats were built in the "old world" style, about 40 feet long with high bows and sterns. They were rigged for sail, but also have small gasoline engines for running when becalmed."

John remembers back in the 1950s when he was working as a helper on John Tooke's boat, the *Jennie Lee*, he would see many of those boats at anchor and the small boats out from them gathering sponges. He estimated as many as 20 boats or more at anchor on many occasions.

Greek sponge boats tied off at Daddy's dock on the river in St. Marks, Florida, 1941.

Mother recalled the Greek boat crews' habit of cooking big pans of food and all would sit around it and eat out of the same bowl. They were very fond of garlic, and, together with the rotting sponges hung out to dry in the hot sun, could often combine to herald their arrival.

Both John and I remember when the Greek boats would come to the dock to replenish supplies. They would give us Greek candy which was much like gum drops with nuts and powdered sugar. I recall an amusing incident when one of the men gave me some coral "trees" which were beautiful pastel colors. I took them home and decorated my bedroom by nailing them to the walls. Since I was only about 11 years old, it didn't occur to me that these "plants" were actually little animals. My parents were not as appreciative of their beauty when they began to rot.

One of the signs of an approaching hurricane, according to Granddaddy, was the Greek boats. He knew by the falling barometric pressure, coupled with the Greek boats heading up the St. Marks River, that a hurricane was likely. With the threat of an approaching hurricane, Newport was always their destination, including all the other boats in St. Marks. Granddaddy depended, at least partially, on the skill of these Greek mariners and said that few could match their knowledge of the sea.

The Pilot

Air planes were all the rage in the '20s. Ivan Munroe, who visited the lighthouse on more than one occasion was an aviation pioneer, known as the "Father of Aviation" in Tallahassee. The Tal-lahassee *Democrat* asserted in 1961 that "Tallahassee's airport and aviation history more or less began with Ivan Munroe." Ivan's *Old Hon* was the first privately owned airplane in the area. (Rogers 107-132)

Old Hon, *from left, Ivan Munroe, Dorothy, Granddaddy and unidentified man, circa 1932.*

Old Hon, *Ivan Munroe's airplane on sand flats at the St. Marks Lighthouse circa 1932.*

Float plane with crew at the St. Marks Lighthouse, circa early 1930s.

Eskimos

Eskimos came down to the lighthouse and stayed for a brief time at the end of the dock. They wore their hoods and heavy clothing and had their dogs with them. I remember Mother saying that the heat had made some of them ill. Unfortunately, we have no information about these people. There are a few photographs of them, but we know nothing about exactly where they came from, or their intended destination. It remains a mystery as to why they would choose to visit us.

Vera and Esther with unidentified Eskimo and dogs at St. Marks Lighthouse, circa 1931.

Eskimos and unidentified man with Aunt Esther, circa 1931.

Eskimo boy.

Chapter 10
<u>HOME SCHOOLING</u>

In Mother's words "Keeping a lighthouse is not a difficult occupation, but rearing eight children at one is..." Without a road and with so many children and chores to keep them busy, education was a problem. During Grandmother's childhood, she and her family had sometimes traveled by horse and buggy the rutted dirt road to civilization. It took two days to reach Fanlew, where the Fine children boarded each year in order to attend school.

Granddaddy was a self-educated man. He read *Time* magazine from cover to cover, as well as the *National Geographic Magazine*. Each evening all the children were required to gather around the radio and listen to Lowell Thomas. Obviously, Granddaddy admired his opinions. If some of Granddaddy's methods bordered on the draconian, it was simply that he placed great value on responsibility, and he lived by that imperative. He was a man who believed that dereliction of duties was a cardinal sin, and that each soul was responsible for his or her best efforts. In keeping with this philosophy, education was essential and basic to all life-long endeavors.

Therefore, for Granddaddy, the only practical solution to educating the children was home-schooling. It was my understanding from Mother that Granddaddy believed that northern schools were superior, but John believes she said that he preferred Northerners because he wanted to insure the children learned "proper English." Mother continues the story.

"...we advertised in several northern papers for a teacher who wished to spend three summer months in Florida at a lighthouse and teach. We were swamped with mail. It was hard to choose someone from all the letters we received.

"When my father decided on a particular one he would write them the details. The teacher had to live in the house with the family and was paid a small salary, part by the government and part by my father. The teacher would arrive by train in St. Marks, and we would meet the new teacher in the small launch. That was always an exciting day for us, meeting the teacher who would be our constant companion for three months."

Mother refers to summer as the school term. There is dispute between her and Edna and Dorothy, who both maintain that school was for nine months. Mother continues,

"We always had a new teacher each summer except for one who came three consecutive summers." This was

Edna Browning Willicombe, a favorite school teacher, circa 1920.

probably Edna Browning Willicombe. In the logs dated September 16, 1922, "Miss Edna Browning Willicombe, teacher, left for her home. Total time spent at station 68 days." The reference to the number of days spent at the lighthouse is another indication that summer was the "school year." It is also worth noting that our Aunt Edna Browning Gresham was born on September 25, 1922. Mother continues,

"We had a room, the living room, made into a class room with school desks and blackboard. We went to class promptly at eight in the morning, and my mother would have our noon meal prepared at 12 o'clock. We returned to the class room at one and stayed until 3:30 in the afternoon. There were always four or five pupils, the smaller children being too young and the older ones going to school or work as they grew up. We were, of course, each in a different grade and would make a grade in three months. We all went through the eighth grade this way. I stayed home longer than the others and just to have something to do went over the 8th grade three times."

"Our teacher, usually a lady, became a dear friend. She not only taught us our books but all about the way other people lived. She would tell us about going to movies, to parties; about neighbors and things that we read about but never did. She taught us girls how to fix our hair pretty and discussed clothes and, if she were young, boys. We, in turn, would take her rowing or sailing, fishing and swimming. Our way of life was as fascinating to her as hers was to us. We often corresponded for years after they returned home."

Since the yearly school term cannot be reconciled, I am taking the liberty of assuming it was summer. The reason is two-fold. It was highly likely that these teachers had regular teaching jobs, and that the summer was free for them to take on this extraneous assignment, as a summer job might be. Besides, swimming and boating would not be the most sought after pastimes in the winter. On the other hand, perhaps when the young girls were in school, that that was the time when Mother was attending business school in Tallahassee and was not aware that the school year had changed.

As regarding the "schoolroom" there are again, differing memories. According to Mother, school was held in the living room. The desks and other accouterments were stored in the basement, which was a small, narrow room under the front porch. Granddaddy later used this area for storage of maintenance supplies. Other memories of the school room had it located in the room across the porch from the kitchen and also in the same building downstairs. (This area was later used during the war as a radio room for the Coast Guard. I remember this, myself. However, I thought that this room was added during the war. Obviously, if it was used as a classroom, I was mistaken.)

Log Entry, Nov. 24, 26, 28, 1932, "Worked on school room."

Log Entry, Dec. 7, 1932, "Painted school room." More reason to believe school took place in the summers?

There were a few male teachers. I vaguely remember Mother mentioning a writer, whose name I never knew; Thad Hollingsworth, and the most favorite of all, our father, Eugene Wilbur Roberts.

Chapter 11
SEAWALLS, ROADS AND THE REFUGE

Erosion on the beach was an on-going problem. Finally, after several log entries about working on the seawall, it was finished on October 17, 1935. Wilbur Roberts helped build it. It was built just beyond the fence about six feet towards the water, running alongside from the front corner of the fence back adjacent to the tower. About midway there was an extension that went down to the water and was used for launching small boats and swimming. During World War II, the

Granddaddy building the seawall, circa 1935.

Coast Guard erected a small lookout flag house alongside the extension. The seawall was supplemented with large boulders that were placed all along the waterfront from the lighthouse all the way down to the canal. There were times, however, when the sea wall was breached, as per Log: Feb. 13, 1936, "Gale from SW, tide 6 feet above sea level. Ten feet of west end of sea wall undermined and considerable damage done to beach."

In 1931 the St. Marks Refuge was established. Paul Kreager from Des

Paul Kreager, the Wildlife Refuge manager. Two of the young girls in the background.

Moines, Iowa, arrived to become the first Manager of the refuge. He left for a brief time for Texas and Washington State but returned and continued as Manager until his retirement. He served longer than any other Manager and, as I recall, had a hard time retiring—announcing his retirement on several occasions only to change his mind. It was obvious to me that his reluctance to leave was indicative of the allure of this place. It had become his home. He and his family, Maribelle and little Paul, became very close to the Greshams, and after Granddaddy retired and settled in St. Marks, Paul also settled in St. Marks right next door.

Maribel Kreager and Little Paul at the Lighthouse, circa 1937.

Log: Nov. 6, 1932, "Mr. Kreager and Roberts visited station." (Note: First mention of Daddy.)

It was also in 1931 that the road to the lighthouse was built. It was built by the Works Progress Administration (WPA), a government agency of President Roosevelt's New Deal. These people were often mentioned in the logs. They also did some work around the lighthouse.

Electricity would not be added until much later, however.

According to Log Entry dated July 29, 1937, not long after the road was built: "...Judging from conversation with Mr. Cochran on July 24, am satisfied that he knows that the power line will not be built to this station by his department. Am making note of this because on July 21, I stated to the visiting lighthouse engineer that I had been assured by Mr. Cochran that the line would be built to the end of the road." Terry Cochran was the Assistant Refuge Manager.

Construction of road to the lighthouse by the WPA, 1931.

Construction of road to the lighthouse, 1931.

Building road, 1931.

Terry Cochran, Assistant Wildlife Refuge manager, circa 1937.

L.B. Turner was the assistant refuge manager for many years following Cochran. He became a good friend of the family, especially, Mother. She told me of an amusing incident when an important official was coming to the lighthouse with L. B. to meet Granddaddy. I have forgotten his mission or who he was, but Mother said that she and L.B. had rehearsed what they would say upon their arrival. When L.B., apparently nervous, appeared with the VIP at the door, Mother said "hello", and L.B. stole her next line and said "Come in."

After the construction of the road, Mother, could now drive the four younger girls to Crawfordville. Since it was a long drive, she would stay all day, sometimes attending school, herself, and sometimes helping the teachers in the classrooms. Thus, the home schooling became a thing of the past. After Mother married, Granddaddy boarded the four younger girls.

Sarah Cochran, circa 1937.

Log Entry, Aug 27, 1940
"Went to Crawfordville to get a place for children to stay during school term."

With the establishment of the St. Marks Wildlife Refuge and the building of the road, there were other changes besides schooling. Although there were obvious conveniences associated with the road, it also brought

Vera Gresham and L.B. Turner,
Assistant Refuge manager, circa
1930s.

L.B. and Frankie Turner, the
former Frankie Moore from St.
Marks, Florida, circa 1930s.

headaches—namely, visitors. Now with easy access, they thronged to the area in droves. Where once the Keepers' home was private and secluded with the occasional visitor by boat, it was now a public domain.

> Log: Aug. 26, 1934, "the 'visiting' problem has become more serious since the road has been built…" This sentiment was echoed in another column by Vera for the Wakulla *County News.*

MANY VISITORS AT ST. MARKS LIGHT
(By Vera Gresham)

"One hundred and four years ago this St. Marks lighthouse was established. I wonder if it is the oldest structure in Wakulla County.

"Since the first of this month we have had over one hundred visitors and admitted forty-eight of them in the tower. Considering the twenty miles of sand road that must be traveled in order to reach this place one naturally concludes that with the road straightened, shortened and hard surfaced as planned and approved by the Federal agency (engineering and construction work are in progress now) that visitors to St. Marks Migratory Bird Refuge and the lighthouse will become a real problem for the officers in charge."

"Visiting the lighthouse on Sundays and holidays is prohibited now, but it is assumed that when the above mentioned road improvements are completed that the lighthouse service will cooperate with the Bureau of Biological Survey in taking care of visitors in every possible manner."

Log Entry, May 25, 1935, "Mr. Ladd of New Port landed 30 people asking that they be admitted in tower—was forced to refuse on account of scaffolding inside of tower and size of party."

Log Entry, May 1, 1936, "Took two hours' time waiting on part of 36 visitors."

Log Entry, Dec. 31, 1937, "Have discontinued waiting on visitors except when convenient and my regular work will not be interfered with. I find that above mentioned arrangements give me the least trouble."

Log Entry, Feb. 6, 1938, "Regular station duties and waited on visitors half the day. Conditions created by so great a number of visitors is beyond my control. Have asked the office for relief and tried to explain several times. Men can't be shooed off like birds. I am behind with my work and have been for more than a year. There seems to be no way out. I am forced to let everything drift."

Log Entry Aug. 25, 1940, "Visitors all day. Estimate more than 250."

Log Entry Mar. 11, 1941 "69 cars visited station. Out of state tags noted, Wisconsin, New York, Arkansas, Michigan, Illinois, Georgia, Alabama, and Massachussetts. 19 persons requested permission to enter tower, more than 20 persons were on the porch at the time. To keep them out of the yard, it is necessary to stand outside from about 11 am to sundown."

According to Mother, the visitor problem was finally alleviated when entering the lighthouse was restricted to Sundays. There was a limit to the number going into the tower; they were invited to sign a registry, and they had to wear white gloves to preserve the integrity of the structure. As a child I do not recall visitors at all.

There was a period around the 1960s that I remember people being everywhere. They were even sunbathing down by the pond where alligators and rattlesnakes lurked. Finally, a sign was erected warning about rattlesnakes, and I do believe that had its intended effect. This was during a time when the light had been automated, and there was no visitor control whatsoever.

Apparently, the road, itself, was not that convenient as per Log dated Sep. 16, 1935. "Went to Tallahassee for supplies; got stuck in mud, lost entire day." However, according to Log, Apr. 4, 1940 "Am assured of rock road to station."

In mine and John's memories, the road to the lighthouse was limestone rock. After rains, puddles would form and splash white limestone all over the car. There were potholes everywhere, and navigating these roads meant winding from one side of the road to the other to try to avoid these holes. It was always obvious if you had been to the lighthouse, as your car would be "whitewashed". To this day, even though the road has been paved for many years, it suffers from a poor foundation of sand and has to be repaired often.

Some of the more amusing entries regarding visitors seemed to indicate there were a number of the unruly and unwashed!

Log Entry: Feb. 9, 1941 "…some extremely vulgar language was used by the crew off the *Larkspur*. They paid no attention to the officer who pleaded with them to stop using such language."

Log Entry: Feb. 11, 1941 "…Admitted 2 drunks in tower."

Log Entry: May 6, 1941 Cleveland Ouzts with the *Franklin D* "spent about 2 hours tied up to dock in boat basin, part of his party of about 10 men were drunk and 6 of them were in my boat. He was requested to get out of the basin and did so without protest."

Chapter 12
<u>VERA AND WILBUR</u>

My grandparents' bedroom was one of the largest rooms in the lighthouse and, like the tower room, held a fascination for me. I,

like most children, had an immense store of imagination and could entertain myself for hours. While the "grownups" were gathered around the kitchen table, I would wander off and often visited the bedroom. It was there that my grandmother had a table filled with family photographs of various sizes and an overflow placed here and there on her dresser. I loved old photographs and was particularly fond of one. It was of Mother and Daddy, taken on October 4, 1936, their wedding day.

Vera and Wilbur Roberts (Mother and Daddy) on their wedding day at the St. Marks Lighthouse, October 4, 1936.

My parents had married at the lighthouse, and the picture was taken outside. Mother was wearing a white dress-length outfit, summery for October, but autumn is often unseasonable beside the warm waters of the Gulf. Daddy, standing a discreet distance from Mother, looked a bit awkward with his arms behind his back and his head tilted to one side, with a silly grin on his face. That was a happy day, and the second marriage in the lighthouse in our family. Grandmother and Granddaddy had married in the living room in 1909. Mother and Daddy wed in the large bedroom next to the living room in front of the fireplace.

According to Mother: "When I was about thirteen years old, we had a young man 21 years old to come teach us one

Wilbur Roberts from Neely, Mississippi.

Daddy's sister, Aunt Esther Roberts McLeod. She also taught at the lighthouse.

summer. He liked it so much at the lighthouse that he stayed on longer and helped with the painting and cleaning. This young man was very serious-minded and strict with us, and I didn't care for him at all. Some ten years later when I was attending business school in Tallahassee he wrote me a letter and asked to visit me. Two years later we were married in the same room at the lighthouse where he had taught me.

Edna remembers Daddy as "being a very kind, well-mannered gentleman...." Her impression was obviously quite different...

Our father, Wilbur Roberts, was from Neely, Mississippi. He had been a bookkeeper with a timber company when first arriving in Tallahassee around 1925. He soon discovered Wakulla County and fell in love with the area. This was mainly because of the excellent goose hunting, as Daddy came from a family of avid hunters. He soon became a resident of St. Marks and began teaching school there.

It was not long after Daddy had established residence in St. Marks that Granddaddy, for the first time, did not advertise for a northern teacher. Instead he offered the position to Daddy. After serving as live-in teacher, the story goes that he liked living at the lighthouse so much that he stayed on for awhile and helped Granddaddy with maintenance. I also have heard it said that he taught more than one school term, and that he was there when Teebee was born. She was born in Tallahassee, and when she was brought home to the lighthouse, Daddy was there on the dock to lift her out of the boat. The memory of his time at the lighthouse is disputed. We do know that he taught at least one school term, and probably more.

After his brief teaching career, Daddy went on to do odd jobs, like fishing, and working for Paul Kreager on the Refuge. There is an amusing story here that I think is worth mentioning. In those days, Refuge employees would often ride horseback into the interior. Without roads, and with the wilderness extending for miles, the rider would stay in cabins at nightfall. One night Daddy heard what sounded like someone calling in distress. He got up, went outside and proceeded to answer by calling out, not realizing at first that he was answering a panther! Apparently, this was his first experience with their very human-sounding scream!

Wilbur Roberts, or E.W. Roberts, as he was known in St. Marks. This picture was taken in the front yard of Mother and Daddy's first home in St. Marks, Florida.

Wilbur later left for awhile for Galveston, Texas, to work on a lighthouse ship. He eventually returned to St. Marks and established a deep sea fishing industry on the river. He courted Mother who was boarding in Tallahassee, attending business school. In seeking her hand in marriage, Granddaddy readily approved on the condition that Daddy provide Mother with a house. He not only complied, buying a brand new "shot-gun" house, but furnished it, and just before the wedding, bought a week's supply of groceries.

Vera Gresham at the base of the tower at the lighthouse, circa 1935. This was Daddy's favorite picture of her.

Recently, John told me something about Daddy that was quite surprising. John likes to write, as I do, and he has written many short vignettes about his youth. One of these is titled "The Magnolia Tree". The following text is from this essay that he wrote about Daddy.

Daddy's first boat, the Annabelle, *circa 1940.*

"THE MAGNOLIA TREE"
By John Roberts

"A beautiful Magnolia tree used to grow on the St. Marks National Wildlife Refuge. My dad showed it to me many years ago, near the edge of Mounds Pond. Even way back then, it was very old and I could tell it could not last much longer. That tree meant so much to my dad and meant a lot to me too after he told me the story of that old magnolia.

"...My dad, in his formative years, migrated from his Mississippi home to Wakulla County, Florida. He soon fell in love with the area and began his life-long profession in the fishing industry at St. Marks. My grandfather, John Y. Gresham, was keeper of the St. Marks lighthouse at that time and was very much impressed with this gentleman from Mississippi. Mr. Gresham had a large family, six girls and two boys, and because of the remoteness of the lighthouse, hired teachers, usually from up north, to live there for a period of time and teach his children. One of those teachers was my dad, and one of Mr. Gresham's daughters, and therefore one of my dad's students, was Vera, my mother. She was eight years younger than my dad. ...

"A number of years passed, and my dad fell in love with her. They were married in 1936 in the living room at the St. Marks lighthouse. She was twenty-three and dad was thirty-one.

Mother and Daddy and me at the lighthouse, 1942.

"Now about that Magnolia tree. Not long before my dad passed away, he took me down to the St. Marks Wildlife Refuge, where the lighthouse is located… Over near Mounds Pond, he pulled off the road and we walked a short distance down a dirt road…

"Then my dad took me into some thick brush and woods, a little closer to Mounds Pond. There he pointed out a very old magnolia tree. There were some dead limbs on the tree, and it seemed to be near death. But it had enough life to be recognizable. I can almost quote my dad: 'Son, when I was a young man, not long before I married your mother, I climbed this tree and took out a nice magnolia flower. I took that flower straight to your mother at the lighthouse, gave it to her, and told her that the magnolia flower is the flower of my home state, Mississippi. …

"I'm so happy that Dad took me to that old magnolia tree all those many years ago. Since then, when able, I have always made it a point to drive down past Mounds Pond to the lighthouse. That magnolia tree died many years ago and although I have looked for it, cannot find a trace. I like to think my parents are in a better place, resting beneath the shade of that beautiful old tree, with flowers in full bloom."

I was surprised, because I had never known that romantic and sentimental side of Daddy's personality. John was indeed privileged to witness it firsthand.

Our house in St. Marks, Florida, from left to right, Edna, Marion, Laura, Dorothy, and me, taken on my fourth birthday, February 13, 1942.

Chapter 13
<u>WORLD WAR II/THE COAST GUARD</u>

There were U-Boats in the Gulf of Mexico during the war, but apparently it was not a serious threat where we were. I would speculate that the Germans were much more interested in the petroleum holding tanks in Texas and Louisiana. In fact, there seemed to be an apparent lack of hostilities in our part of the Gulf, as the light in the tower was never extinquished during the war. There was one exception not related to the war, however.

> Mar. 17, 1942, "A bunch of night herons (25) were blinded by the light and were unable to get away from it, flying around the tower and screaming for more than an hour. The light was turned off for a few minutes to allow them to go on their way."

Sometimes desperate circumstances called for desperate measures!

During World War II, a Coast Guard station was established at the lighthouse. There was a small house at the end of the road for Lieutenant Whitsel, and a barracks built alongside the house on the other side. The Coast Guard boys were duly noted in the logs, most of them arriving in early 1942. Their names, according to the log book, were Jimmy Barr, Paul Hobush, McGowan, E. F. Jones and Cook. That did not include all of them. I also remember one named Myrle, but cannot remember his last name. For some reason he and Jimmy Barr are the ones I remember. One of the boys, Gus Kannwischer, from New York, married Dorothy's best friend, Nelly Dolby from St. Marks, and of course he became a friend of the family.

Granddaddy was compelled to join the Coast Guard and wear a "monkey suit" as he called it. He was second in charge under Whitsel. (NOTE:) Conversion from USLHS to USCG was established in 1939.)

Log Entry: June 27, 1941, "Went to Tallahassee to have photos made in connection with induction into the Coast Guard, also to take oath before a Justice."

On that day "that will live in infamy," Granddaddy used the Log entry of Dec. 7, 1941 to express his patriotism—"Japs started raising HELL. We will finish with them during 1944."

Granddaddy holding John at the lighthouse in May or June of 1942.

Log Entry: May 13, 1942, "Went to St. Marks and Tallahassee. The Tallahassee trip was strictly personal due to major operation on a daughter, spent 1 hour in Tallahassee." (Note): This was John's birthday. Back then a caesarian delivery was considered major surgery, and a second caesarian birth, especially dangerous.) Obviously, all went well.

John Roberts, St. Marks, Florida, 1955.

Log Entry: May 16, 1942, "Took McGowen to USCG 361, traded for Thomas." (NOTE): Almer P. Thomas

Log Entry: Dec. 11, 1941, "Met 2 enlisted men in Tallahassee at 2:50 pm, Mr. Hobush and Barr. Left Tallahassee 3:30 pm, arrived on station 5:00 pm. Watches will be 12 noon to 12 midnight for Mr. Barr and Hobush with Keeper on duty and subject to call anytime."

> (NOTE): James "Jimmy" Barr and Paul Hobush apparently were derelict in their duties as per Log: Apr. 17, 1942 "Barr and Hobush continue to ignore orders to wear uniforms, lax in attendance to watch."

Log Entry: Aug.4, 1942 "Garrot "The Cook" starts today."

Log Entry: Jun 6, 1942 "Barracks finished except for plumbing. Men moved in."

Log Entry: Jul 16, 1942 "Bozant, Walter T., SC1, USCG, arrived on station at 2 pm."

Log Entry: Aug 16, 1942 "Bozant, Walter T. returned to duty. This is a strange man."

Log Entry: Sep. 28, 1942, "...Evidently I'm under the direction of Lt. Whitsel..." Do I discern a note of resentment?

Log Entry: Nov. 5, 1942, "Telephone service 'direct' with base in St. Marks was established today." (NOTE:) There was a base located on the river in St. Marks at Outz's dock, later known as "Wilson's" dock.

Log Entry: Nov. 24, 1942 "Visited base. Was authorized to buy Chief's uniform by Lt. Whitsel."

Log Entry: Dec. 15, 1942 "The cook knows about as much about his job as I about flying a plane."

Log Entry: Dec. 31, 1942 "…we have lots to be thankful for—there is nothing to indicate that this war will end during 1943 but lets pray and work, nothing is impossible with God's help" (Signed by Keeper J.Y. Gresham and he subtracts 1918 from 1942 to reflect his duty at the station for 24 years.)

There was a small room below the room across the porch from the kitchen. It extended out beyond the front porch. The upper room was used for storage and sometimes as an extra bedroom for Alton and J.Y. or for teachers. Beneath it was a room at ground level. It was sometimes used as a schoolroom, according to Edna and Dorothy. I remember it, though, as a radio room for the Coast Guard. I remember standing behind the chair of one of the boys as he talked funny using such words as "foxtrot" and "x-ray," etc. The Coast Guard boys took turns using the tower as a lookout. They also had a little house overlooking the Gulf where they flew the flag. It was also used as a lookout.

When not watching the coast, the boys helped Granddaddy with the chores, especially the never-ending painting. It was my understanding that they loved their assignment. They were all from the North (for some reason it seemed that Southerners were sent north, and vice versa, perhaps to keep them from returning home?) These fellows were evidently so taken with their assignment that every one of them moved to Florida after the war. Many would return for visits on occasion. I would suppose, too, that the proximity of such pretty girls was an inspiration to them, even though they could only look from afar. I do have a photograph that Mother took of all the boys standing against the fence with all four of my young aunts and myself. I would guess, at times, some cautious intimacy was allowed.

The four young girls from left to right, Dorothy, Laura, Marion, and Edna. Standing behind them I remember only the one on the far left, Merle, and the third one from the right, Jimmy Barr. That's me on the cook's shoulder.

The exception, of course, was Nelly and Gus. Nelly Dolby was part of an influential family in St. Marks, and her father had been Granddaddy's best friend before Harry Dolby's untimely death. Nelly was a friend of the family, and, as the story goes, Nelly, came down to the lighthouse for a visit one day and saw Gus standing on a ladder painting one of the walls of the lighthouse. Nelly was tall, and finding someone taller than she was difficult, especially back then when most women and men were shorter. Gus Kannwischer was over six feet tall. Nelly took one look at him and said "There's the man I'm going to marry!" So one rainy day in St. Marks, she and Gus dropped by our house for a visit. I remember she was so excited, running towards the house shouting "We just got married!" Gus and Nelly settled in Tallahassee and raised a family there.

I would like to insert at this point a couple of pleasant memories associated with our Coast Guard boys. During the war, everything was rationed, as so much had to go to support the military. John was an infant and Daddy became upset when he could not buy milk for him due to a depletion at the store. So, in a huff he took off for the lighthouse to get the milk. They were so kind, offering much more than he requested.

Another episode occurred one day in St. Marks when we were driving up to the house. As we approached we saw a young Coast Guardsman leaving the house and driving off in his jeep. During those days no one had to lock their doors, even at night. When we entered the house, there on a living room chair was a doll for me.

The Coast Guard boys, of course, had a mascot. He was a beautiful Spitz named "Pooch". However, the mosquitoes in Florida are particularly hard on dogs,

Grandmother and Granddaddy in the living room at the lighthouse. Note the deep window seat and the curved wall of the tower room. This was a posed picture for some article, circa 1945.

because they can cause heartworms and death. They were particularly bad at the lighthouse. So the boys gave the dog to John.

104

Chapter 14
RETIREMENT/THE COAST GUARD

Grandaddy retired in 1949, and he and Grandmother settled in St. Marks where he enjoyed working in the yard, planting trees—some shipped to him from Hawaii by Marion (then Marion Patronis) where she lived at the time. He was a true horticulturist and created a beautiful yard full of various stands of exotic trees, mingled with the local Pines and Magnolia. Honeysuckle covered the backyard fence, and I remember the Japanese Magnolia and Dogwood, harbingers of spring.

Grandaddy passed away in May of 1957, and Grandmother continued living in the little house in St. Marks until her health failed, and she had to live out her life in a nursing home. The house stayed in the family for a few years longer. George, my husband, and I moved there with our two children when we moved back to the area from Hawaii. We stayed at Grandmother's house until we could find one of our own and renovated it so that it could be put on the market.

(NOTE:) Keeper's Logs during the rest of the 1940s and early 1950s during Uncle Alton's tenure, were not located in the National Archives by the staff. We will continue with log entries beginning in 1951, and I will rely upon my memories of the two years that Uncle Alton served as keeper.

After Granddaddy retired, the Coast Guard took over the lighthouse, rotating the keepers every two years. It was fortunate that Uncle Alton, who was in the Coast Guard at the time, was able to take over as the first Keeper. His two-year tenure began with Granddaddy's retirement in 1949 and continued through 1951. He and his wife, Connie, and their two children, Sonny and Joann moved in during the summer of 1949. Our family always spent the summers in St. Marks, so it was wonderful going to the lighthouse

Mother and Edna at Young and Lela's retirement home in St. Marks, Florida, circa 1952.

Picnic in the backyard of the grandparents' retirement home in St. Marks. From left to right, Lela, Vera, Connie (seated), Uncle Alton's wife, and Teebee. Edna is standing behind Mother and Aunt Connie, circa 1951.

Gathering of the clan at the grandparents' retirement home in St. Marks, Florida, 1950. From left to right, Granddaddy, John, Daddy, Elmo, Dorothy holding Lamar, Marion, holding Bill, Laura, Grandmother, Mother, and me.

to visit our cousins. The many happy hours spent at the lighthouse were extended to two more wonderful years.

Mother and Alton were born only 14 months apart, and were almost like twins—not just in age—but had very similar personalities and thought alike. In their declining years, they would tease each other about who would "go" first, finally deciding they would depart this world the same day. Interestingly, that's what they did! They both passed away on July 23, 1999. Alton was in Tallahassee and Mother was in a nursing home in Newport News, Virginia.

At the end of Uncle Alton's tenure, (July 1, 1951) other Coast Guardsmen took their turns caring for the light. Log: Jul 1, 1951, "Officer in Charge: William F. Barry" (The term "Keeper" was no longer used)

Officer Barry was followed by: Donald D. Luedke, BM2, USCG, Officer in Charge,—Jan 1952 to 1953; Log, Robert C. Hogenmiller, BM2, USCG, Officer-in-Charge—May 1953.

Log: May 25, 1953, "0700, departed to search for drowned man in area of #1 light, St. Marks river. 1000, picked up body and turned it over to the Sheriff of Wakulla County."

Uncle Alton in his Coast Guard uniform about the time he became the first Coast Guard lighhouse keeper of the St. Marks Lighthouse in 1949.

Log: Jan 24, 1954, "Camechis, Johnnie V., SN(BM), USCG, reported in for permanent assignment to duty." (NOTE:) This man is subordinate to the Officer in Charge.

Log: May 11, 1954, "1500, departed in CG 25679 with Sheriff Farrell from Wakulla County to search for the body of Cleveland Reed of Roswell, GA, who drowned 8 miles south of St. Marks Light Station. Unable to locate body."

Log: Jun 22, 1954, "Camechis departed, transferred to Miami, Fl, for permanent duty."

Log: Aug 8, 1954 "Found dead possum in cistern, drained and cleaned. Washed with Clorox."

Log: Oct. 23, 1954, "1430, the body of Bruce Cannon, Albany, Georgia., was brought in to the lighthouse by fishermen. The man died of a heart attack. Called local law officers. 1500, law officers arrived 1600, and removed body from the station."

Log: Mar. 14, 1955, "Tore out part of wall in kitchen to make an archway to living room. Archway completed."

Log: Apr 8, 1955, "Comeaux, Kenneth V., FN, USCG, departed. Transferred to CGC NEMESIS, St. Petersburg."

Log: Apr. 10, 1955, "Barnard, Jimmy D., SN, USCGR, arrived for assignment to .duty." Hogenmiller was still O-in-C.

Log: May 1955, New O-in-C appears, Melvin Long, BM1 USCG.

Log: May 6, 1955, "Hogenmiller, Robert C., BM2, transferred to CGC NEMESIS, St. Petersburg, Fl."

Log: Aug 6, 1955, "1600, Sardegna, Carl A., SN, reported aboard for duty."

Log: Oct 12, 1955, "Sardegna transferred to CG Depot, St. Petersburg, Fl."

Log: Oct. 11, 1955, "Jones, Raymond J., FN, reported for duty"

Log: Apr 21, 1956, "Bateman, Hugh W., FN reported for duty

Log: Jun 9, 1956, "Received telephone call from Elmer E. Oliver, owner of the fishing boat *Daily Double*, that Charles Collett of Alpharetta, Georgia, jumped overboard from his boat and drowned near St. Marks river light #8 at 1725".

John and I helped daddy on the docks during the summers, and I was there the day that Elmer Oliver, Mother's first cousin, brought his boat, the *Daily Double*, in. It was a terrible tragedy that I will always remember. The boy, about my age at the time, was a sleep-walker and on the way in had gone below to take a nap. His father was standing near the door, but Charles bolted out the door in a fast run, put his hand on his father's shoulder and went overboard. "Uncle Elmer" as we called him, never took another party out; sold his boat, and went back to fishing for a living.

Log: Jun 10, 1956, "Dragged river for body from 0500-1500. Negative results."

This continued every day through June 13th and included divers. The Coast Guard stood by to assist the divers.

Log: Nov. 12, 1956, "Milton, John L., SN reported for duty."

Log: Feb. 4, 1957, "Kudrick, Albert, BMI, USCG, reported on board as new O-in-C."

Log: Feb 6, 1957 "0745, received call from Mrs. Tooke, St. Marks, reporting overdue motor vessel *Jennie Lee.*

1130, called air station, St. Pete, requesting plane search for motor vessel *Jennie Lee*. 1510, St. Pete air station located *Jennie Lee* in tow of motor vessel *Hermosa*, proceeding to St. Marks."

I remember some of the Coast Guardsmen who kept the light during those years (one couple spent their honeymoon there), and I became acquainted with a young couple from Miami whose little boy was drowned in the pond behind the house. I remember only their first names, but according to the Log dated March 14, 1955, the door to the front bedroom from the kitchen was installed. The logs mistakenly record that the door was to the living room, but it was actually to the front bedroom. When visiting them they mentioned adding the door so that they could be closer to their son, Johnny, as that bedroom was apparently his. Since the logs do not reflect their names or this sad occurrence, memory is all I have to go on. Sadly, life on the water can be tragic.

The lighthouse ceased being manned sometime in 1960 and has been automatic ever since. After the war, the CO's small house and the barracks disappeared, and after the light became automated, the lighthouse, the grounds and other outbuildings fell into disrepair. There was even a brief time when there was some talk of doing away with the lighthouse entirely. This, of course, was very unpopular, especially among the Greshams. In recent years the Coast Guard Auxiliary used the house to operate radio equipment, but they have since departed.

Today there is renewed interest in the historic value of the lighthouse among the local residents, and there is an effort to restore it to its original design. On my last visit there, I noticed that the porch once again ran the length of the house. John told me that they were also restoring the inside to reflect the way it was when Granddaddy was there. There is a lookout platform out by the road and some information regarding the surrounding terrain and wildlife. It is peaceful there—not too many visitors. All you can hear is the wind in the Palms. In the heavy silence, though, there are many voices.

The St. Marks Lighthouse as seen from the lookout where Granddaddy's garage used to be. Photo circa 1980s or 1990s.

An aerial view of the St. Marks Lighthouse, circa 1990s.

BIBLIOGRAPHY

Chabek, Dan. Lakewood *Sun Post*, October 25, 1990. Reprinted with permission.

Cipra, David. *Lighthouses, Lightships, and the Gulf of Mexico.* 1997, McCarthy, Kevin. *Florida Lighthouses.* 1993.

Civil War Naval Chronology, 1861-1865, Part II, page 69, 167.

Clifford, Mary Louise, J. Candace Clifford. *Women Who Kept The Lights.* Williamsburg: Cypress Communications, 1993.

Davis, T. Frederick. "Destruction of Port Leon." *Florida Historical Quarterly*, Vol. 24.

Fitch, Franklyn Y. *The Life, Travels and Adventures of an American Wanderer*, original publication 1883, publisher John W. Lovell. General Books publication, 2009, pages 6, 7 and 8.

Magnolia Monthly, Vol. II, No. 12, December, 1964.

Port Leon Gazette. 9/15/1843. *Magnolia Monthly*, Vol II, No.5, May 5,1964.

Revels, Tracy J. *Grander in her Daughters, Florida Women During the Civil War*, University of South Carolina Press, 2004, pages 71, 127.

Rogers, William Warren. *Outposts on the Gulf*, University of West Florida Press, 1986, pages 10, 85 and 125.

_____. *A Historic Sampler of Tallahassee and Leon County*, Florida Historical Press, 2005, Chapter 11, pages 107-132.

Shofner, Jerrell A. *Daniel Ladd, Mercant Prince of Frontier Florida*, University Press of Florida, 1978.

INDEX